TILES AND TILEWORK
OF EUROPE

TILES AND TILEWORK OF EUROPE

Alun Graves

V&A Publications

Cover illustrations: Front *See* 88–9; Spine *See* 18; Back *See* 125b.

Endpaper: Taken from the catalogue of F. St John, G. Barr,
and Co. 1844. V&A.

Frontispiece: The Palácio da Mitra (now the Casa do Gaiato)
at Santo Antão do Tojal in Portugal. Courtesy of Hirmer
Verlag, Munich.

Illustrations on pp1–6: 1 *See* 49t; 3 *See* 95br; 4t *See* 100; 4c *See* 70;
4–5 *See* 53t; 5t *See* 16; 5c *See* 144; 6tl *See* 151bl; 6tr *See* 42–3; 6b
See 56t

Abbreviations: t = top, b = bottom, c = centre, l = left, r = right

V&A Publications
160 Brompton Road
London SW3 1HW
www.vam.ac.uk

Contents

Acknowledgements

In writing this book, I am indebted to Jennie Stopford, John Mallet, Michael Archer and Jennifer Opie, who read those chapters relevant to their own areas of expertise and made a great many helpful suggestions. Particular thanks are also due to Reino Liefkes, who supported the project throughout, and who read the entire manuscript. I would also like to thank Alfonso Pleguezuelo and Chris Cox for the generosity with which they shared their time and expertise, and the Cañada Blanch Foundation, who funded a research trip to Spain. Many others have in various ways provided assistance. Among them are Timothy Wilson, Paul Drury, Nick Wickenden, Ed Gibbons, Juame Coll, Robert Elwall, Melissa Bromley, Wilhelm Joliet, Wilfried Hansmann, Marie-Dominique Nivière, Vicent Estall i Poles, Dominic Crinson and Fiona Hayes. My thanks go to them, and to everyone else who has helped. I am especially grateful for the generous assistance with translations provided by Judith Belleteste and Alexander Gunn. The production of the book could not, of course, have happened without the constant input and support of my colleagues at the V&A, nor without the opportunities afforded by a secondment to the museum's Research Department, during which the bulk of the text was written. As well as those of my colleagues already mentioned, I would like to thank Mary Butler, Geoff Barlow, Monica Woods, Carolyn Sargentson, Malcolm Baker, Juliette Hibou, Kellie Daniels, Terry Bloxham, Emily Howe, Robin Hildyard, Oliver Watson, Vicky Oakley, Fi Jordan, Juanita Navarro, and all others who have contributed, including everyone in Ceramics and Glass. Special thanks are also due to Christine Smith for her superb photographs, to Bernard Higton for his excellent design and to my editor, Rachel Connolly. Finally, I would like to thank Julie Taylor for her constant encouragement and support.

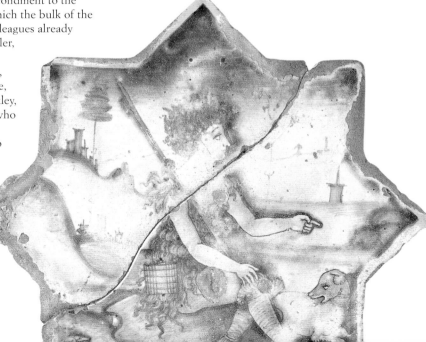

Introduction

CERAMICS have been used as decorative architectural components since antiquity. As early as the reign of Djoser (c.2630–2611BC), the Egyptians employed small greenish-blue glazed tiles in the decoration of the subterranean chambers of the great Step Pyramid at Saqqara. In the ancient Near East, where the art of brick-making has its origins, the Assyrians and Babylonians both used architectural ceramics to striking effect. Finely painted figurative tiles of the ninth century BC are known from the Assyrian cities of Ashur and Nimrud, while moulded glazed bricks formed the spectacular Ishtar Gate of Babylon (now in Berlin's Pergamonmuseum). Built around 600BC, this remarkable edifice was decorated with a series of lions, bulls and dragons in relief. However, the use of glazed bricks and tiles gradually died out in the Near East, prior to its dramatic revival in the hands of Islamic potters from the ninth century onwards. In Europe, the beginnings of a tradition of decorative tilework emerged soon after, with the appearance of lead-glazed floor tiles at sites in the north, and the introduction of new ceramic techniques and practices from North Africa to Islamic Spain.

The aim of this book is to provide an outline of the historical developments in the production and use of tiles in Europe, from these medieval origins to the present day. The subject is itself vast, but made more so by the fact that it cannot be meaningfully discussed without reference to the history of ceramics, to architecture, to design, and to the panoply of political, cultural, social, economic and scientific forces that shape how and where we live.

Although the Romans operated major brick and tile industries, their principal forms of architectural decoration were painting and mosaic. The tiles they produced were largely for roofs or wholly utilitarian functions such as constructing flues. Though not necessarily lacking in decorative merit, such tiles are nevertheless beyond the scope of this book. The class of tiles dealt with here are those used to cover floors, walls, ceilings and other architectural features such as fireplaces, the production of which has tended to be more closely allied to the fine ceramic industries than to brick-making. Such tiles (unlike those used to cover roof pitches) have in common the fact that they are laid with edges abutting so as to form a continuous, unbroken and essentially flat layer of cladding. Despite forming an integral architectural feature, such a layer is nevertheless non-structural. An essential characteristic of the medium is the regularity of the modules with which the surface is covered. Squares, rectangles and hexagons can each be used alone within tiling schemes.

Other shapes such as octagons cannot, although the gaps between rows of octagons can be filled with squares. Thus various tilework patterns emerge. This ability for regular shapes to cover a surface in its entirety also usefully distinguishes between the tile-mosaic dealt with here, and tessellated mosaic, which is not. In the former, various geometrical shapes are cut so as to fit perfectly together. In the latter, complete coverage is achieved only by virtue of the small unit size of the tesserae, with any slack being taken up by varying the width of the mortar joints. Of course, much tessellated mosaic is made up of glass or stone rather than ceramic.

The flat surface of tiles provides an ideal base for decoration. Numerous ceramic techniques and an endless variety of styles have been employed over the centuries to this end. Some designs are complete on a single tile; others are formed by repeating elements of a pattern over a number of adjacent tiles. Panels of tiles are also frequently used as a base for pictorial compositions which pay little regard to the modular nature of the medium. In all cases, however, single tiles are essentially fragments of a larger whole, and knowledge of how the tiles were originally set is thus essential to our appreciation of the decorative impact of the scheme and our understanding of its function. Tiles that remain *in situ* or that have been accurately recorded through paintings, drawings, photographs or other documents, are therefore vital pieces of evidence. One further point regarding decoration perhaps needs to be made. Despite the prevalence of decorated tiles in this book, plain tiles would frequently have dominated production. While this imbalance is in part simply a reflection of aesthetic merit, it is also a function of the higher survival rates of objects upon which a greater value is placed. References to undecorated tiles produced within the same industries as those under discussion have therefore been included as a reminder of this wider context.

In a general history such as this, constructed around the development and dissemination of techniques, attention is invariably focused on innovation, and a closer and more detailed approach has been taken to follow the introduction of new practices. Accordingly, as techniques become firmly established, the emphasis shifts to a more general discussion of production and use. As a result, there are plenty of tile manufacturers whose names go unrecorded in these pages, and those with a particular fascination for one firm or another may not find what they are looking for. What I hope will be conveyed, however, is a sense of the richness and longevity of the traditions of tilework in Europe, bearing in mind that these are only a part of what is an ancient and global phenomenon.

NORTHERN · MEDIEVAL TRADITIONS

Pavements of decorated ceramic tiles are a creation of the Middle Ages, their invention providing yet another way in which to add to the richness and splendour of the great churches of the period. Their early use was almost exclusively ecclesiastical, though from the mid-thirteenth century royal patronage also played a considerable part in their development and proliferation. From this time, substantial industries became established, producing tiles in considerable quantities and exploiting expanding markets. A range of decorative techniques was employed by the medieval tile-makers, with different traditions developing in different regions. Though the practice of laying lead-glazed floor tiles spread throughout northern Europe, the longest and richest traditions are to be found in France and England.

Bricks and roof tiles were standard products of the Romans. Yet following the collapse of the Western Empire, the production of ceramic building materials all but ceased in north-west Europe. Only in the mid-twelfth century did a major revival of these industries occur, and it was in this period that the manufacture of decorated floor tiles became established.

An earlier series of late Anglo-Saxon tiles is, however, known from a number of ecclesiastical sites in England. Tiles from Bury St Edmunds, St Albans, Winchester and other sites in the south-east appear to have been made at a common centre in the Winchester area, while others found at Coventry and York are of local manufacture. Nevertheless, they share similar characteristics, most being decorated with simple linear patterns in low relief. In many cases the decoration has been enhanced by the use of glazes of different colours, ranging from yellow through to a deeper brown or olive-green, applied to the different compartments of the relief designs. While it remains unclear precisely where these tiles were originally set within the churches, it is likely they faced walls or stepped areas close to the altar. The series as a whole probably dates from the tenth or eleventh century, and perhaps the early to mid-eleventh. As yet there is little evidence to suggest any continuity of production between these and the relief tiles of the twelfth century. This may simply be due to the lack of surviving material. Plain-glazed tiles found in a late eleventh-century context in a monastic building of Westminster Abbey, along with some unusual tiles from Lisieux in Normandy of around the same date, suggest that production was taking place in this period. By the late twelfth century, however, three distinct types of decorated tile were being produced.

Twelfth-century tiles with decoration in high relief are known from sites in England, Alsace, Denmark and the Czech Republic. Among the earliest is a group of paving tiles from the chapter house of St Albans Abbey, dating from around 1160 (fig. 1.2). These large, square and rectangular tiles are decorated with complex foliate designs in relief under a clear lead glaze. Comparable tiles have also been found at Hertford Priory and Wymondham Priory, both dependencies of St Albans. Also of the third quarter of the twelfth century are the tiles of the church of Sainte-Foy at Sélestat in Alsace (fig. 1.3). The Cistercian abbey of Sorø has, meanwhile, yielded the earliest known tiles from Denmark, dating from the late twelfth century. There are not necessarily any direct links between the relief tiles of

Left: 1.1 The pavement of the refectory at Cleeve Abbey exemplifies the more widespread use of tiles within the cloistral buildings of monasteries by the late thirteenth century (see p16). English Heritage Photographic Library.

Above: 1.2 A border tile fragment from the chapter house of St Albans Abbey. The twelfth-century floor was laid in a series of panels edged with border tiles, the overall layout of which perhaps guided processional movement within the building. Width 15.9cm. V&A. C.66-1933.

1.3 Centaurs are depicted in high-relief on large octagonal tiles from the church of Sainte-Foy at Sélestat in Alsace, dating from around 1150–75. Other tiles from the site were decorated with similarly fantastical creatures and foliate ornament. Width 23.2cm. V&A. 150-1902.

these various regions, and their origins remain tantalisingly obscure. Nevertheless, their spread broadly follows the Rhine, and coastal regions beyond. Thus, in the early thirteenth century further examples of relief-decorated tiles appear in Switzerland, the Low Countries, and also in Scotland, where the discovery of a tile kiln at the site of North Berwick nunnery has proved the local production of tiles of an extremely high quality (fig. 1.4). North Berwick was at that time an important port and the point of disembarkation for pilgrims en route to St Andrews.

Some of the early relief tiles with fine or particularly high-relief decoration may have been moulded. However, the standard technique involved stamping the design into the surface of the tile with a carved wooden block while the clay was still soft. In the earliest Swiss tiles, from the Cistercian abbey of St Urban near Zofingen and other related sites, multiple small stamps have been used to decorate the same tile, thus enabling different designs to be made from different combinations of stamps (fig. 1.5). This type of tile, which was normally left unglazed, was produced in quantity in the north-west of Switzerland and neighbouring regions of Germany.

A second type of decorated floor tile to emerge in the twelfth century has been found at a number of sites across France and England, with additional examples in Belgium and Hungary. These were decorated with simple linear designs, either incised by hand using a sharp point, or impressed into the surface of the tile in counter-relief using a stamp. This latter technique, though clearly comparable to the production of relief tiles, nevertheless seems to have been derived from the hand-incised method, as identical designs appear on tiles of both techniques at certain sites. The series is primarily though not exclusively associated with Cistercian monasteries, where the simple geometrical designs and the plain dark brown or black glazes seem to have conformed to the strict principles governing decoration adopted by the Order. The bulk of the series dates from the period 1190–1220, though hand-incised tiles from Orford Castle in Suffolk can be firmly dated to as early as 1165–7.

By far the most prevalent type of tile pavement in late twelfth-century France was, however, tile-mosaic. Such pavements were constructed using tiles of various shapes, each of a single colour. Most shapes were cut from rolled slabs of clay before being fired. Simple shapes could first be marked out on the slab by impressing their outlines with a length of string or wire, while more complex or curved shapes were scored around a template before being cut out. Sometimes small square tiles were fired as larger glazed slabs on which deep lines had been scored, these allowing the tiles to be broken apart. This technique was in fact

1.4 A fragmentary tile from North Berwick nunnery. Although they cannot be dated with certainty, the North Berwick tiles perhaps represent the earliest decorated floor tiles in Scotland. Width 15.2cm. V&A. 5669-1901.

1.5 A mid-thirteenth-century tile of the Saint Urban type, made at Freiburg im Breisgau in Germany. The different decorative elements have been impressed with separate stamps. Such tiles seem to have been set in walls as well as floors.
24.4cm sq. V&A. 112-1902.

widely used throughout the medieval period to produce triangular pieces from standard square tiles (fig. 1.19). The colours of the mosaic tiles were achieved through the combination of different clays and glazes: a clear lead glaze over a plain red earthenware tile would appear reddish-brown, while the addition of copper oxide to the glaze would produce a dark-green or black tile; yellow or light-green tiles could similarly be made by first coating the tile with a layer of white clay. Pavements combining yellow and dark-green or black tiles were the most commonly employed.

The model for these floors can be found in the marble and stone *opus sectile* pavements laid in prestigious sites in France throughout the twelfth century. For example, tile-mosaic found at the church of Saint-Ouen in Rouen is identical in design to an earlier *opus sectile* pavement from Rouen Cathedral. By-and-large, the designs of the floors, which relied for their effect on the shapes of the tiles, were restricted to relatively simple geometrical patterns. They must nevertheless have appeared striking and highly colourful. So much so, in fact, that when they were laid at Cistercian sites in France in the early thirteenth century they seem to have caused something of a scandal. It may well have been a pavement of this type for which the Abbot of Pontigny was reprimanded in 1205, the removal or alteration of the offending floor being demanded. However, any attempts to restrict the use of particular types of floor tiles by the Cistercian Chapter General seem to have been abandoned during the second quarter of the thirteenth century, and it is possible that the practice of laying tile-mosaic spread from France to England through connections between Cistercian houses.

One of the earliest sites with tile-mosaic in England was Beaulieu Abbey in Hampshire, dating from around 1227. This paving may have been contemporary with some of the

Left: 1.6 A splendid mosaic roundel in the south transept of Byland Abbey, composed of tiles in a range of curvilinear shapes. Originally yellow or green, much of the glaze or slip has worn from their surfaces. Tiles set on the step risers are better preserved.

Below: 1.7 A section of the pavement in the south transept at Byland, showing different mosaic arrangements.

celebrated mosaics found at a series of sites, including several Cistercian abbeys, in the north of England and Scotland. The tiles at all the northern sites were made by the same workshop. Those at Fountains Abbey, North Yorkshire, were probably laid between 1220 and 1247, and some fragments have been reset close to the site of the high altar. At Byland Abbey, also in North Yorkshire, substantial sections of the mosaics remain on site (figs 1.6 and 1.7). Their relatively good condition makes them by far the most important surviving example of this type of paving. Some pieces of particularly complex mosaic roundels were discovered at Meaux Abbey, East Yorkshire, and the kiln site where the tiles were made has been excavated at nearby North Grange (fig. 1.32). The Meaux tiles are known to date from the period 1249–66 and may have been the last of the series. The mosaic tiles from Newbattle Abbey in Scotland could have been made in Yorkshire and shipped northwards up the east coast.

During the second quarter of the thirteenth century, a new type of tile with decoration inlaid into its surface using clay of a contrasting colour made its appearance. The inlaid tile is one of the great inventions of medieval craftsmen. It enabled complex and intricate patterns, including figurative designs, to be placed on standard square and rectangular tiles that could be reproduced in quantity and laid with relative ease. Comparisons have been drawn between inlaid ceramic tiles and the stone slabs inset with

mastic or lead found at sites such as the cathedral of Saint-Omer. However, the origin of the inlaid tile can be found within the development of ceramic tiles themselves.

In Normandy, makers of tile-mosaic in the Lower Seine valley began to experiment with new decorative techniques early in the thirteenth century. An occasional refinement made in the production of mosaic pavements was the removal of a cavity from the centre of some tiles, these being filled with correspondingly shaped pieces of a different colour when the tiles were laid. However, on tiles found at the cemetery of Saint-Maur in Rouen, the simple designs (in this case trefoils placed on triangular mosaic tiles) were reproduced by cutting the design through a layer of white

1.8 The great roundel from the abbey church of Saint-Pierre-sur-Dives, as published by Alfred Ramé in 1852. Narrow bands of plain tiles probably once separated the bands of inlaid tiles. V&A (National Art Library).

clay applied to the surface of the tile, so as to reveal the red clay beneath. Meanwhile, other mosaic tiles from Rouen have unusual decoration in the form of blobs of white clay applied to discs impressed in their surface. Though no true inlaid versions of the tiles with inserted pieces can yet be associated with mosaic floors in Normandy, they later appear in conjunction with their derivatives in the north of England. Similar experiments also seem to have taken place at Saint-Benoît-sur-Loire near Orléans. However, the most striking piece of evidence to suggest the advent of the inlaid tile comes from the Cistercian abbey of Fontenay in Burgundy. Here, line-impressed counter-relief tiles of simple geometrical designs co-exist with versions produced with the same stamps in which the impressions have been filled with white clay. Thus, with suitable stamps available, inlaid tiles could be made by a relatively simple modification of an existing process. These tiles cannot be dated more accurately

than around 1220–50, and it is not clear whether they represent the invention of the inlaid tile, whether the technique was borrowed from elsewhere, or whether the process was simultaneously evolved through experiments at different sites.

Whatever the exact course of development, and there are clearly many lost pieces of the jigsaw, the first great realisation of the new technique to survive in Normandy was the pavement of the Benedictine abbey of Saint-Pierre-sur-Dives (fig. 1.8). The spectacular roundel relaid in the chapter house in 1924 is made up of tiles from as many as four roundels originally set in the choir of the church. The tiles from the roundel and others from the abbey have a striking repertoire of inlaid designs, including lions, griffins, double-headed eagles and addorsed birds as well as a range of scrollwork and foliate motifs and arcading. As a pink-firing clay was used to form the body of the tiles, an

1.9 A section of the pavement from the King's Chapel at Clarendon Palace.
The tiles were excavated at the site, having fallen from their original location on
the first floor of the building. The inscription assembled from the scattered
letter tiles is not original. © The British Museum.

additional thick layer of red-firing clay has been applied to provide better contrast with the inlay. This additional step has also been reversed to produce tiles with a red inlay on a white ground. The date of the Saint-Pierre-sur-Dives tiles is uncertain, though must fall somewhere in the second quarter of the thirteenth century. Nevertheless, it seems certain that the inlaid technique was firmly established in Normandy during the 1230s, and it is probable that it was introduced to the Île-de-France from there during that decade. Square inlaid tiles found in association with tile-mosaic at the abbey of Saint-Germain-des-Prés in Paris and the nearby Cistercian abbeys of Maubuisson and Royaumont are the earliest known examples in that region. The products of a single workshop, they must date from around 1235–45. Interestingly, all three sites had close royal connections, and the pavements, which seem to have included separate panels of mosaic and of inlaid tiles, can be assumed to have been those favoured by the royal court at that time.

The influence of Normandy can also be seen in the sudden emergence of the new technique in Hampshire, Dorset and Wiltshire (the 'Wessex' region) in the early 1240s. Inlaid tiles found at Winchester Castle can be linked to entries in the royal accounts referring to pavements laid in 'the king's hall' and 'the chapels and the king's and queen's chamber in the castle' during 1241–2. These are the earliest known products of an itinerant workshop which went on to make tiles for a number of sites, including Beaulieu Abbey and Christchurch Priory, but most famously for Clarendon Palace near Salisbury. Here the tilers erected a kiln within the palace complex (fig. 1.31) and produced the splendid pavement of Henry III's (r.1216–72) private chapel, ordered by the King in 1244 (fig. 1.9).

Meanwhile, an entirely separate group of tiles can be linked to Henry's extensive building projects at the palace and abbey of Westminster. As early as 1238 a tile pavement was laid in a private chapel adjacent to the King's new chamber, known due to its mural decorations as the Painted Chamber, at the Palace of Westminster. In 1241, an order was made for tiles for the Painted Chamber itself, and a further pavement was laid there in 1249. Nothing remains of these floors, though a magnificent pavement in the chapter house of Westminster Abbey has survived largely intact (fig. 1.10). This was completed by at least 1259. The tiles in the chapter house are extremely finely decorated and carry a range of designs including the royal coat of arms, human figures, animals, birds and fish, as well as foliate and architectural motifs. These are laid as a series of long panels each separated by a row of border tiles.

Another group of exceptional tiles similar in design to

1.10 The floor of Westminster Abbey Chapter House. The pavement's survival is largely due to its having been boarded over. When uncovered in 1841, the tiles aroused great antiquarian interest. English Heritage Photographic Library.

those of Westminster has been found at Chertsey Abbey in Surrey and other sites. These were initially produced as complex inlaid tile-mosaic, though later the designs were adapted to more standard shapes (fig. 1.11). The extraordinarily fine decoration of the tiles seems to have been achieved by pressing the clay into a form with a carved wooden block at the bottom, rather than using the block as a stamp. The most celebrated of the Chertsey tiles are two sets of large pictorial roundels: a series depicting combat scenes likely predates another illustrating the romance of Tristram and Isolde (fig. 1.12). The border tiles made to frame the roundels are no less splendid, these being decorated with fantastical creatures and foliage. Smaller roundels decorated with the signs of the zodiac and the labours of the months are among other tiles from Chertsey, as are a large group of finely decorated standard square tiles. Production of tiles for Chertsey seems to have begun around 1250, and continued for much of the rest of the century. The later tiles from the series, at least, are known to have been made on site at the abbey. Similar tiles were also used at Hailes Abbey in Gloucestershire and at Halesowen Abbey in the West Midlands. Here they were made around 1290–8.

Owing to the similarity of the Chertsey tiles with those of the chapter house at Westminster, and the slightly surprising choice of designs for an ecclesiastical setting, it seems probable that the designs for the tiles were in fact

1.11 A tile from Chertsey Abbey, dating from around 1260–90. Originally, the tiny roundels and foliate sections of the design were produced as separate mosaic elements. 14.0cm sq. V&A. C.9-1918.

originally made for pavements ordered by Henry III at Westminster, and it is possible that those of the Painted Chamber were of this type. Unlike the tiles from Winchester and Clarendon, however, the Westminster-Chertsey tiles have no clear antecedents in France. Nevertheless, their sudden appearance in England in a fully evolved form suggests that French expertise was involved.

That royal patronage should have played such an important role in the introduction of the technique to England is perhaps unsurprising. Henry was a French-speaking Plantagenet with numerous connections in France, and showed considerable admiration for the art and architecture of the French court. His programme of improvements to royal residences seems in fact to have been prompted by his marriage to Eleanor of Provence in 1236.

Until the mid-thirteenth century the manufacture of floor tiles had proceeded by way of small-scale specialised production carried out by tilers working either on an itinerant basis (such as Winchester-Clarendon tilers) or supplying only a very limited number of sites within a small area (such as the tilers working in Paris around 1235–45). However, by this time, the market for decorated tiles had begun to change, no doubt partly in response to the wider decorative possibilities of the new inlaid tiles. Until around 1240, decorated floor tiles had essentially been used only at the major religious houses, and then usually only within the churches themselves. However, after this date they appear in royal palaces, and not merely in chapels but also in domestic settings within the residences. From the later thirteenth century they were increasingly to be found in the castles and manor houses of the nobility, in the cloistral buildings of abbeys as well as their churches, and perhaps most importantly in terms of the market expansion, in parish churches. This clearly offered new opportunities for tilers and resulted in different patterns of working and an increased scale of production.

After 1250, the output of certain workshops, the number of sites they supplied, and the length of time they could sustain production from a single settled tilery, increased significantly. Changes in production in the Wessex region are indicative of the new and expanding markets. In 1250, tilers returned to Clarendon Palace in order to make a new pavement for the Queen's Chamber. Once again drawing upon the repertoire of motifs established in Normandy and exemplified by the pavement at Saint-Pierre-sur-Dives, the tiles of the new Clarendon floor established a particular stock of designs that were endlessly repeated at sites throughout the south-west of England and South Wales (fig. 1.13). Whether or not the tilers had established a permanent tilery at this point is unclear, though by around 1260 they were certainly working from one fixed location, perhaps in the Clarendon area. The workshop produced tiles in vast quantities and must have remained in operation beyond 1280, around which time were laid the tiles of the retrochoir of Winchester Cathedral, the largest section of medieval tile paving to survive *in situ* in England, and a further surviving floor in a chapel (now the vestry) at Christchurch Priory. Another contemporary Wessex pavement, that of the chapter house of Salisbury Cathedral, was removed and replaced with reproductions during Sir George Gilbert Scott's restorations of the cathedral in 1860–78.

Other tile workshops were in operation in Wessex by the last quarter of the thirteenth century. The large heraldic tiles bearing the royal arms, the arms of Poitou, and the arms of Clare, laid in a pavement which survives *in situ* at the site of the refectory at Cleeve Abbey in Somerset, are among the products of just such a group (figs 1.1 and 1.14). These designs were probably first made to commemorate the marriage of Henry III's nephew Edmund of Cornwall to Margaret de Clare in 1272. Another, possibly related, group of tilers established a workshop at Nash Hill in

Above: 1.12 Inlaid tile mosaic from Chertsey Abbey, dating from around 1250–60 and incorporating large roundels depicting King Richard I and Saladin from a series of combat scenes. These and most of the other roundels of this series were fired as four quarter sections, though in this reconstructed section of paving they have been fixed together. Total width approx. 80cm. © The British Museum.

Below: 1.13 A section of paving from Keynsham Abbey, Somerset. The designs on the tiles are almost indistinguishable from those used at Clarendon in 1250–2. Total width approx. 74cm. V&A. 1125 to DD-1892.

Wiltshire in the late thirteenth century. Here, decorated floor tiles were produced on an independent commercial basis alongside pottery and roof tiles until around 1325, by which time the demand in the region seems to have been largely exhausted.

A comparable expansion of production to that of Wessex occurred in the Paris region after 1250. Here, a new and distinctive style of pavement was developed composed of square panels of rectilinear tile-mosaic. Inlaid tiles were sometimes incorporated into the mosaic or used as borders. Both the mosaic and inlaid tiles were distinctive in terms of the techniques employed in their manufacture. The mosaic was derived entirely from square tiles of around 12cm using the method of deeply scoring the tiles before firing. The inlaid tiles, on the other hand, were unusual in that the white clay was introduced in the form of a slip (clay in suspension in water), a technique that became prevalent in the fourteenth century. Pavements of this type are known from ten sites in the region, including the abbeys of Saint-Denis and Saint-Germain-des-Prés, where such a floor was laid in the chapter house around 1273. Production by the workshop responsible was sustained until around 1285, at which time the tilers dispersed. One group apparently moved to Canterbury, perhaps as a result of a commission to make a floor for the cathedral. Here, a section of rectilinear tile-mosaic laid in the Corona Chapel around 1290 has survived *in situ*. The Parisian tilers worked from Tyler Hill outside Canterbury, a site where the manufacture of pottery and roof tiles was already practised. Although the production of tile-mosaic was not sustained, a significant inlaid tile industry was established there.

In addition to Canterbury, an unmistakable Parisian influence can be seen in a late thirteenth-century pavement at Charlieu Priory in Loire. Meanwhile, yet another group of tilers from Paris seems to have joined an established workshop in the Garonne valley in south-west France. Having been based in Bordeaux around 1260–70, this workshop had since become itinerant, and was working progressively eastwards at sites along the valley. A magnificent pavement at Grandselve, laid around 1285 and typical of the earlier products of the workshop, was composed of a series of large rectangular panels of diagonally set inlaid tiles decorated with fleur-de-lys and other bold and simple Gothic motifs. At Moissac, however, panels of rectilinear tile-mosaic made a sudden appearance in a pavement laid around 1290 (fig. 1.15).

The Garonne valley workshop was exceptional in the south of France where few lead-glazed tiles of any kind were produced. However, from the middle of the thirteenth century the manufacture of inlaid tiles had become firmly established across northern France and Belgium. In addition to Normandy and the Île-de-France, Picardy, Champagne, Burgundy, Artois and Flanders each had its own industry with its own distinctive regional characteristics. It may in fact have been increased competition from tiles brought by river to Paris from Normandy and Champagne that prompted the departure of the Parisian tile-mosaic workshop. Meanwhile, the products of a prolific workshop operating in Anjou during the third quarter of the thirteenth century shared certain characteristics with those of Wessex, and were likely derived from a common source in Normandy. A large roundel found at the church of Cunault closely resembles that of Clarendon Palace.

In southern England, too, the production of inlaid tiles was widespread in the late thirteenth century. As well as the industries based at Tyler Hill and in the Wessex region, commercial production was also taking place in Essex, the South Midlands and London. At Danbury in Essex, the site of a tile factory operating from around 1280 to 1330 has been extensively excavated (fig. 1.30). Here, as was increasingly typical, the manufacture of decorated floor tiles was a relatively small part of a substantial industry dominated by roof tile production.

In some instances, commercial production of tiles appears to have followed in the wake of important monastic commissions. This was the case in the South Midlands, where tilers who had been employed in the production of a pavement for the new east end of the church at Hailes Abbey around 1278, went on to make tiles

Left: 1.14 A late thirteenth-century tile from Lyme Regis, decorated with the double-headed eagle of Richard of Cornwall. The design is among those present in the Cleeve Abbey pavement. 14.0cm sq. V&A. 1310-1892.

Right: 1.15 The pavement (now destroyed) of Moissac Abbey, as reproduced in the Bulletin Archéologique in 1894. The panels of rectilinear mosaic are typical of the earlier Parisian workshop and its derivatives. V&A (National Art Library).

on a commercial scale. At Hailes the tilers deliberately exploited the effects achievable through the modification of firing conditions. Red 'oxidised' tiles were alternated in the pavement with grey 'reduced' tiles, produced in a kiln starved of oxygen in the latter stages of firing. A commercial workshop likely to have been based in London in the later thirteenth century was considerably less skilled, their products (known confusingly as 'Westminster' type) being of universally poor quality. Nevertheless, a pavement of their tiles found in the hall of a merchant's house in the City of London demonstrates the wider market that inlaid tiles by then enjoyed.

1.16 Two *sgraffito* tiles from Tring Church in Hertfordshire. This technique, in which the design is cut through a layer of white clay, allows decoration of considerable refinement to be produced but is unsuited to large-scale manufacture. Width of each 35.9cm. V&A. C.469 & 470-1927.

Despite the explosion in popularity of the inlaid tile, and its eminent suitability for mass production, other techniques were used on occasion for the production of two-colour decorated tiles. An unusual though not unique mosaic pavement was laid in Prior Crauden's Chapel at Ely in Cambridgeshire around 1324, parts of which have survived *in situ*. Specially shaped *opus sectile* tiles are used to depict Adam and Eve and a series of heraldic lions, these having been covered with a layer of white slip through which additional decoration was incised. Other mosaic tiles have line-impressed decoration designed to imitate more complex mosaic, this also enhanced by areas of slip. Incised (*sgraffito*) decoration was also used to produce the magnificent early fourteenth-century tiles from Tring Church in Hertfordshire, these depicting the Apocryphal Gospels of the Childhood of Christ, and derived from a series of manuscript illuminations (fig. 1.16). Owing to the nature of the decoration and their lack of wear, the tiles were probably set in the wall of the church. The lively drawing, imbued with immense character, has made them one of the masterpieces of medieval ceramic art. The technique, though unusual, was not without precedent. A splendid series of tile tombs from the abbey of Jumièges in Normandy, made around 1213–39 and now known only through a series of drawings, may well have had incised decoration; other Norman tile tombs of the early fourteenth century certainly employed the technique.

In the middle years of the fourteenth century, the availability of tiles made as special commissions, be they inlaid or produced in some other fashion, decreased markedly. This was a direct consequence of the Plague, which struck England in the winter of 1348. Communities were decimated and the income of the aristocracy substantially reduced through lost taxes. Yet in some ways the Plague strengthened the hand of the surviving craftsmen, who were now better placed to work on an independent basis and to charge higher prices. The industries of the time thrived, and even the Royal Clerks of Works turned to a commercial tilery to supply their needs. This was the massive tile factory at Penn in Buckinghamshire, which produced inlaid floor tiles alongside roof tiles from around 1332 until at least 1388. Henry Tyler, Simon the Pavyer and John the Tyler, who were all farmers as well as tilers, were already among the wealthiest inhabitants of Penn and Taplow when they were assessed for tax in 1332. Penn supplied its products along the Thames Valley as far as London, and numerous churches and important buildings in the region were paved with their tiles. No fewer than 45,000 Penn tiles were laid under the auspices of William of Wykeham, the Royal Clerk of Works from 1356, during his first year in office alone.

Among the early products of the factory were tiles decorated with heraldic and figurative designs (fig. 1.17), but from around 1350, simple repeating ornamental patterns became standard. These were often symmetrical so as to simplify the task of laying the tiles. The size and thickness of the tiles was also reduced,

1.17 A tile from Reading Abbey, produced by the Penn factory. 11.7cm sq. V&A. 1330-1892.

1.18 A sixteen-tile group from Ulverscroft Priory in Leicestershire, made by the Nottingham workshop, probably in the mid-fourteenth century. Tiles for the priory were also supplied by Chilvers Coton. Total width 56.5cm. V&A. C.97 to O-1981.

1.19 Tiles from Castle Acre Priory, made at Bawsey. Some have been scored diagonally before firing to enable them to be broken into triangular sections, though perhaps due to a surplus of these when the floor was laid, they have been left whole. Each approx. 10.2cm sq. V&A. 1033 to 1042-1905.

enabling larger quantities to be produced and profits to be increased. Despite the conscious drive towards mass production, the Penn tiles were generally of good quality, a deterioration apparently only occurring in the final period of the factory's operation.

The commercial production of inlaid tiles was also taking place at a number of sites in the Midlands in the fourteenth century. At Chilvers Coton in Warwickshire, successive tile kilns were constructed at an established pottery production centre. Similarly in Nottingham, tile manufacture was linked to that of pottery (fig. 1.18). Meanwhile, both inlaid and line-impressed tiles were produced at Repton Priory in Derbyshire in a kiln presumably built to serve the monastery, but which also supplied tiles elsewhere in the

1.20 Line-impressed counter-relief tiles of around 1250–75, found at sites in the Rhineland: (l-r, t-b) Strasbourg; the Deanery of St Stephen's in Mainz; the Stadionsche Domherrenhof in Konstanz; St Andrew's Church in Worms. Each approx. 13.3cm sq. V&A. 218, 173, 99 & 177-1902.

region. A substantial industry producing line-impressed counter-relief tiles also developed in Cheshire in the later fourteenth century, with related production being carried out in Dublin and Drogheda in Ireland.

The dominance of line-impressed tiles in the north-west of England was matched by a preference for relief and counter-relief tiles in East Anglia. A major industry was operating at Bawsey near King's Lynn in the years around 1376, producing small, square relief tiles decorated with a mix of heraldry, animals and birds, geometrical and foliate motifs and inscriptions (figs 1.19 and 1.33). Pale and dark glazes were used to produce a mix of red and dark-brown tiles that on occasion were laid in chequerboard arrangements. The products of the Bawsey kiln were distributed widely in East Anglia, especially in the more populous northern areas, but also to the south and east of King's Lynn where the tiles could be readily transported over the region's extensive network of inland waterways. Numerous parish churches were supplied, as well as a number of larger religious houses including Castle Acre Priory.

The regional preference for relief tiles in East Anglia perhaps owed something to links with Continental Europe, for in the Rhineland and to the east, various relief and counter-relief techniques maintained their dominance and inlaid tiles do not appear to have been made. In addition to the relief tiles of the St-Urban type, line-impressed floor

tiles became popular in the Rhineland during the second half of the thirteenth century (fig. 1.20). These were typically decorated with bold, linear designs of hunting scenes, figures and heraldic animals, as well as foliated roundels, these being spread over four tiles. Such tiles have been found over a wide area, though principally in the Rhineland cities of Konstanz, Strasbourg, Mainz, Frankfurt, Cologne and Dusseldorf.

Tiles for use in closed wood-burning stoves were also produced in great quantity in Germany (see pp68–9). In the later fourteenth and the fifteenth century these usually took the form of niches made from half-cylinders. Around 1500, however, these began to be replaced by rectangular panel-type tiles with decoration in relief. The front surfaces of these tiles were moulded, after which deep flanges were applied to their backs to increase heat-retention. Coloured

1.21 A polychrome stove tile depicting Faith ('Gelaube') and bearing the date 1561. Made in Cologne, the tile is one of a series depicting the Virtues and Liberal Arts, after engravings by Sebald Beham. Height 31.8cm. V&A. 2992-1853.

lead glazes (often green) had long been used to enhance the tiles. However, during the sixteenth century, polychrome stove tiles painted with a variety of different coloured glazes became popular (fig. 1.21). The preference for relief decoration in the production of stove tiles seems to have been shared by the makers of floor tiles, who began to make regular use of (monochrome) coloured glazes during the fifteenth century (fig. 1.22). Floor tiles produced in Germany at this time, such as those from Cologne, remain predominantly Gothic in style. However, Renaissance ornament became widespread in the mid-sixteenth century, both in the decoration of floor and stove tiles.

Line-impressed tiles like those of the Rhineland are also known from the Netherlands, however both inlaid and mosaic tiles were more extensively employed here. In Utrecht, for example, the predominant technique from the late thirteenth to the mid-fourteenth century was that of rectilinear tile-mosaic, made using the same methods as the earlier Parisian workshop. This use of complex tile-mosaic appears to have given way to a preference for a simpler

1.22 A tile from Cologne decorated with a lion rampant, dating from around 1450–1500. The glaze would originally have covered the entire surface. 13.0cm sq. V&A. 75-1902.

arrangement of standard square tiles in plain colours, normally yellow and dark green or black, generally laid in a chequerboard fashion. From the late fourteenth until the mid-sixteenth century, plain tiles of this type were exported in vast quantities to England and Scotland from Flanders and also by way of Middleburg in Holland. An early example of such a pavement has survived *in situ* in the Consistory Court of York Minster. Floors of 'Flemyshe pavynge tiles of greene and youllow' ordered by Henry VIII for the halls of Hampton Court and Christ Church, Oxford, perhaps represent the latter end of the trade.

The mass importation of plain tiles from Flanders seems to have satisfied much of the demand for floor tiles in England. Meanwhile, many of the locally produced inlaid tiles of the fifteenth century were of fairly poor quality, no doubt the products of non-specialist tileries or potteries. Those of the commercial tilery at Little Brickhill in Buckinghamshire were probably better than most, though were nevertheless of relatively inept design. However, monastic patronage in the mid-fifteenth century resulted in something of a rebirth of inlaid tile manufacture in the Severn Valley, with finely decorated tiles being made to special commission for a number of sites. Richly decorated tiles with fine architectural detail and intricate inscriptions were made at Great Malvern Priory for use in the church (fig. 1.23). As well as laying pavements, large, rectangular inlaid tiles were set on the reredos, where they remain *in situ*. The tiles for the priory were made between around 1453 and 1459. At the same time, the Great Malvern tilers were also producing a splendid pavement for the abbey in Gloucester (now Gloucester Cathedral). Tiles in the pavement, a section of which survives before the high altar, bear the date 1455 and the name of the abbot, Thomas Sebrok, at whose behest they must have been laid.

A related group of fine late fifteenth and early sixteenth century tiles was produced in South Worcestershire. Examples have been found in parish churches in the region, but the most spectacular floors were produced for sites in Bristol and South Wales, a notable group appearing as far afield as

1.23 A set of tiles from Great Malvern Priory. The top tile includes the inscription '36 H VI', dating the design to the thirty-sixth year of the reign of Henry VI, that is, 1458–9. Width 16.0cm. © The British Museum.

1.24 The Canynges pavement from Bristol, as published by Henry Shaw in 1858 when the floor was still in situ. Most of the tiles are now in the British Museum. V&A (National Art Library).

Dyfed, of which a pavement at St David's Cathedral has in part survived. The tiles for these sites must have been transported by boat down the Severn and along the Bristol Channel. The most complete pavement to have been preserved comes from a house which stood in Redcliffe Street in Bristol, known by the name of its former occupant, William Canynges. The floor, which occupied a first-floor room, must have been laid sometime after 1481 (fig. 1.24). Similar tiles were produced for St Augustine's Abbey in Bristol, while the same workshop also appears to have been commissioned to make tiles for Edward Stafford's castle at Thornbury (fig. 1.25), as well as for Hailes Abbey in Gloucestershire.

Finely decorated tiles were likewise produced in Yorkshire and Dorset in the early sixteenth century for use at monastic and ecclesiastical sites. The dissolution of the monasteries from 1536, however, removed one of the tilers' principal client groups. For a time, demand came from secular patrons. The tiles made for William Sharrington in 1550–3 for his new residence at the former abbey at Lacock in Wiltshire are notable for their Renaissance inspired decoration. Similarly, a series of Netherlandish inlaid tiles decorated with inscriptions, imported in the years around 1550, seems to have primarily been destined for major private residences (fig. 1.26).

The production of inlaid tiles in France had in fact experienced something of a revival under secular patronage during the first half of the sixteenth century, prompted by the building of numerous châteaux. Fine inlaid tiles were produced for the châteaux of the Loire, and most notably

the royal château of Blois. Meanwhile, some exceptional line-impressed tiles from Neufchâtel-en-Bray in Normandy were decorated with fine Renaissance-style heads (fig. 1.27), with comparable designs also appearing on square tiles made in Sussex. Nevertheless, the production of decorated lead-glazed tiles waned in the later sixteenth century in both England and France. From then on, it was only the persistence of minor local industries that perpetuated the traditions. A series of seventeenth-century relief-decorated tiles from Devon are known from a number of churches in the region, while inlaid tiles seem to have been an occasional product of the Donyatt pottery in Somerset during the same period. A somewhat larger but equally outmoded industry producing inlaid tiles primarily for use in fireplaces persisted in Flanders even until the nineteenth century (fig. 1.28). By then, however, and after centuries of neglect, inlaid tiles were set for a revival.

1.28 An inlaid tile from Flanders or Artois, probably of the eighteenth century. Such tiles represent a late manifestation of the technique prior to its industrial revival in the nineteenth century. 14.5cm sq. V&A. C.59-1978.

1.25 Tiles bearing the arms of Edward Stafford, Duke of Buckingham, made for Thornbury Castle by tilers working in the Worcester area. Construction of the castle began in 1511, and was incomplete when Stafford was beheaded by Henry VIII in 1521. Each 17.1cm sq. V&A. 1094 to C-1892.

1.26 Dutch tiles from the parish church of Edmonton, London. The inscription (here incomplete) reads, 'Die tyt is cort, die doot is snel, wacht u vā sonde, soe doedi wel' (Time is short, death is swift, beware of sin, so do good). Each 14.6cm sq. V&A. 782 to D-1864.

1.27 Line-impressed tiles made at Neufchâtel-en-Bray in Normandy. This technique was not widely used in France. Width of each 12.1cm. V&A. 1766 & 1767-1892.

A Medieval Tile Factory

The factory site would have contained a number of structures. First was the workshop where the tiles were made. This was normally a timber-framed building with a tiled or thatched roof. A much less substantial building was used to stack the tiles while they dried; no more than an open-sided, timber-framed shed. The tiles were fired in an up-draught kiln of rectangular form, constructed from bricks and roof tiles. At the base of the kiln, normally below ground level, was the furnace. Above this, a series of arches supported the oven floor. The walls of the kiln probably rose no higher than about 1.5m. Kilns built by itinerant workshops may only have been worked for a short period of time. Elsewhere, individual kilns might have remained in a serviceable condition for upwards of twenty years. Some workshops may have used a factory site intermittently, perhaps based on the availability of fuel from coppiced woodland, which in the fourteenth century was harvested at roughly seven-year intervals.

The production of tiles was a seasonal activity. Lack of dry fuel, difficulties in drying tiles and the risk of frost damage to unfired tiles would have hindered year-round manufacture. An Act of Parliament of 1477 stipulated that the clay was to be dug by 1 November, turned before the beginning of February and not made into tiles before March. Tilers probably had some other occupation during the winter months, possibly agricultural. The laying of tiled floors, which may often have been carried out by the same craftsmen, might also have taken place in winter; the royal accounts record that pavements at Winchester Castle were laid between 'Christmas and the Close of Easter' of 1241–2.

Regardless of whether a workshop was settled or itinerant, the siting of a tile factory was governed by the same basic requirements: ready supplies of clay, sand, water and kiln-fuel (usually wood) were essential. The clay used to form the tiles was normally dug close to the factory site, from square pits or long ditches. The white clay used to decorate the tiles, and other materials used in smaller quantities such as lead, could be obtained from farther afield. Settled workshops also required good access to transport by land or water to distribute their products.

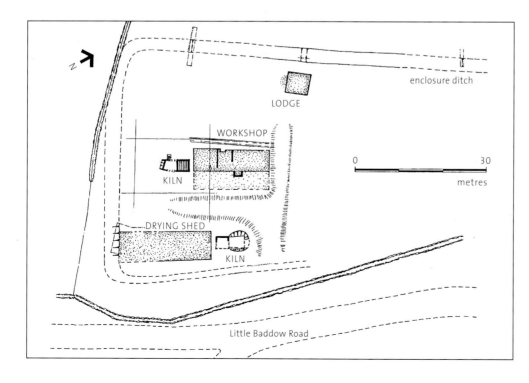

Above: 1.29 A miniature from a fifteenth-century Netherlandish bible, apparently depicting brick-makers in Egypt, though in reality based on a local medieval brick or tile workshop. The form of the kiln is somewhat fantastical, but the activities being carried out reflect those routinely performed. British Library.

Left: 1.30 The layout of the fourteenth-century tile factory at Danbury. Despite the presence of some sort of lodge, there is little evidence to suggest that medieval tilers lived at the site of their workshops. Chelmsford Museums. Reproduced with kind permission of Paul Drury.

Above: 1.31 The remains of a tile-kiln built by itinerant tilers within the palace complex at Clarendon in 1244. Once the commission had been fulfilled, the kiln was demolished and another building erected on the site. © The British Museum.

Right: 1.32 A drawing illustrating the probable form of the kiln at North Grange, Meaux, based on fragments excavated in 1958. A tiler would have to climb over the walls into the kiln in order to stack the tiles ready for firing. Once loaded, a temporary roof of clay and tiles would be constructed. © The British Museum.

1.33 The distribution of products from the late fourteenth-century tilery at Bawsey in Norfolk reflects the extensive network of waterways in the region. An error made in the production of this particular Bawsey design provides a reminder of the processes involved: when the wooden stamp was carved, the design was not reversed, resulting in the inscription 'Thomas' reading backwards on the finished tiles. 9.8cm sq. V&A. 5663-1901.

SOUTHERN MEDIEVAL TRADITIONS

While tile-making in northern Europe developed alongside the great Gothic cathedrals and religious houses, the origins of tilework in the south are associated with a very different form of architecture. In the Moorish palaces of the Kingdom of Granada in southern Spain, tiles were an integral feature. Intricate tile-mosaic created shimmering surfaces of brilliant colour in an architecture both monumental and ethereal. The styles and techniques that evolved alongside this architecture were to dominate tile production in central and southern Spain until the sixteenth century. Also in the south, but more importantly in Valencia and Catalonia, the technique of painting decoration onto a white tin glaze was adopted. The subsequent use of this technique elsewhere in Europe dominated tile production for centuries.

The origins of tilework in Spain are inextricably linked with its Islamic past and the cultural traditions which persisted following Christian reconquest. All but the most northerly regions of the peninsula had come under Islamic control following the Muslim invasion of 711. Originally ruled from Damascus, Spain quickly gained a measure of independence, with the fully autonomous Caliphate of Córdoba being established in 942. However, the fledgling Christian states of northern Spain had already begun to gain ground, and from the eleventh century the *Reconquista* pushed the frontier with Islamic Spain further south. Toledo fell in 1085, prompting the intervention of the Moroccan Almorávides who took control of Islamic Spain, or *Al Andalus* as it was called. They were succeeded in the mid-twelfth century by the Almohades, who fought against the reconquest with renewed energy. However, following the decisive battle of Las Navas de Tolosa in 1212, substantial Christian gains were made, particularly by the dominant kingdoms of León and Castile, and Aragón. Valencia was reconquered in 1238, Seville in 1248, and

soon only the Kingdom of Granada remained under Muslim rule. Though technically a vassal of Castile, the Kingdom of Granada (or Nasrid Kingdom) was effectively independent and flourished for much of the next two centuries, only giving way to the militarism of Ferdinand II (r.1479–1516) and Isabella (r.1474–1504) in 1492. The kingdom was by no means isolated, but surrounded by a broad frontier-land over which it had a strong cultural influence.

Although much of Spain was under Christian rule, the majority of craftsmen were of Moorish descent, and perpetuated their customary styles and techniques, creating an art and architecture termed *mudéjar*. Indeed, the areas where tile-making traditions developed most strongly were by-and-large those where Muslim cultural influence was most pronounced, such as Granada, Málaga, Seville, Toledo and Teruel. The expulsion of Moorish peoples from Spain occurred only in 1609.

The practice of decorating walls with glazed ceramic tiles, which reached such levels of brilliance in medieval Spain, has its origins in the Near East. From there it spread west along the northern coast of Africa, through Egypt, Tunisia and Morocco, perhaps reaching Spain with the Almohades. In the late twelfth and early thirteenth century, monochrome glazed slabs were used as isolated decorative elements in the exterior walls of towers such as the Giralda and the Torre del Oro in Seville, while glazed pottery items were used to similar effect in the thirteenth-century *mudéjar* towers of Aragón.

Right: 2.1 The fourteenth-century Salón de los Embajadores (Hall of the Ambassadors) in the Palacio de Comares of the Alhambra (see p31). © Raghubir Singh.

Above: 2.2 A fragment of fourteenth-century tile-mosaic (*alicatado*), assembled from cut pieces of tile on a backing of plaster. Width approx. 29cm. V&A. 300-1870.

Left: 2.3 The Patio de las Doncellas in the Alcázar, Seville, photographed by Charles Clifford around 1855–60. The Islamic and *mudéjar* architecture of Spain became a source of fascination for British writers and artists during the nineteenth century. V&A. 35:456.

Above: 2.4 The dazzling *alicatados* of the Patio de las Doncellas in the Alcázar, Seville, dating from around 1366.

However, tilework first became a major architectural element in the palaces and residences of Andalucía. Writing before 1240 of the pavements of the houses of *Al Andalus*, Ibn Sa'id stated: 'they have a great variety of tones, and replace the coloured marble used by Orientals to embellish their houses'. This probably refers to the tile-mosaics known as *alicatados*, which, in addition to their use on floors, were employed to brilliant effect as wall decoration, most notably in the palaces of the Nasrid kingdom. An important early example can be found at the Cuarto Real de Santo Domingo, a thirteenth-century *villa* in Granada. Here, wainscots of tile-mosaic take the form of interlaced geometrical bands dominated by cool colours,

primarily blue, turquoise, white and black. Further panels set in the entrance are extraordinarily intricate, incorporating epigraphic decoration in Kufic and *neshki* scripts. The technique used in the production of the mosaics involved cutting various polygonal shapes, or *aliceres*, from already fired earthenware slabs, each glazed a single colour (fig. 2.2). These cut sections were then laid face-down and backed with plaster. Once dry, the panels thus formed could be fixed to the walls. The procedure required skilled craftsmen, but the results produced were spectacular, the close-jointing that could be achieved with this method adding to the apparent brilliance of the colours of the finished surface.

The most splendid manifestations of the technique are perhaps to be found in the extensive tilework of the palaces of the Alhambra in Granada (see pp44–5). Constructed by successive Nasrid sultans during the thirteenth and fourteenth centuries, the most richly ornamented of the palaces were those built under Yusuf I (r.1333–54) and Muhammad V (r.1354–9 and 1362–91). Their architecture is magnificent, balancing space and light, and combining sumptuous interiors with open spaces where fountains and water-channels add sound and motion, and pools carry the reflections of surrounding buildings. The interior walls, as well as those of courtyards and patios, were richly ornamented with tile-mosaics forming wainscots about five feet high (fig. 2.1). In marked contrast to the arabesque curves of the stucco on the walls above, the mosaics were of strongly geometrical design, their patterns including networks of stars and of interlaced bands. As well as wainscots, tile-mosaic was used to decorate floors, door and window frames and other architectural features.

It is perhaps surprising how closely the architecture and decoration of the Alcázar in Seville, reconstructed between 1364–6 for the Castilian monarch Pedro the Cruel (r.1350–69), resembles that of the Alhambra palaces (figs 2.3 and 2.4). Such similarity serves to reinforce the dominance of *mudéjar* craftsmen in Christian Spain. Other Sevillian nobles copied the decoration of the Alcázar and used tile-mosaic at their own residences. Examples include the palace of the Ponce de León family, now the Casa Olea, the palace of the Duke of Béjar, now the Palace of Altamira, and the palace of the Coronel family, now the Convento de Santa Inés. The technique was also employed in the decoration of numerous Sevillian churches of the fourteenth century, such as Omnium Sanctorum, Santa Marina and San Gil, where the high wainscot of tile-mosaic has survived. The quality of Sevillian tile-mosaic became well known, and it was employed on buildings across

2.5 Andalusían tiles of the 'Niebla' type, dating from the late twelfth or thirteenth century and made using the *cuerda seca* technique. Each approx. 6.4cm sq. V&A. 910 & 911-1897.

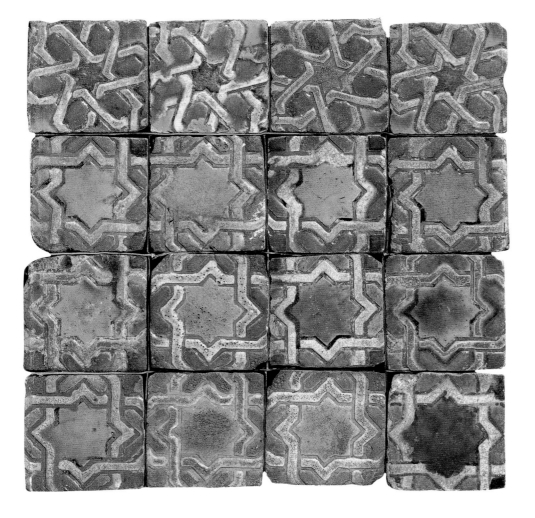

2.6 Two *cuerda seca* tiles from the Convento de Santa Paula in Seville, made around 1500. Of Gothic design, the tiles are part of a group of three in which the shield is supported on either side by an angel. Height approx. 26.0cm. V&A. 1362 & 1367-1892.

southern Spain. Craftsmen from Seville are also known to have travelled to fulfil commissions elsewhere in the country. In 1378–9, for example, Garcí and Lope Sánchez worked on the chapel of San Miguel Arcángel at the cathedral in Zaragoza. Also in the late fourteenth century, Sevillian craftsmen produced the tile-mosaics for the Convento de las Dueñas in Salamanca and the royal chapel of the Mezquita in Córdoba.

From the early thirteenth century, Valencia was also a centre for the production of tile-mosaic. The technique seems to have been learnt under Almohade rule, prior to the reconquest of the city in 1238. Unlike Granada and Seville, its primary applications during this early period appear to have been in the decoration of fountains, water-channels and other garden features, though it is likely to have also been used to cover walls. A fountain from this period survives at the Royal Palace of Valencia, while another, now in the Museo Nacional de Cerámica, was found at Plaza de la Figuereta in Valencia in 1908. Both are decorated with small geometrically-shaped monochrome tiles of different colours. Unlike the standard practice in southern Spain of cutting pieces from already fired slabs, these mosaic tiles were cut before firing.

The use of geometrical monochrome tiles persisted in Valencia until the early fifteenth century, particularly for flooring. The 'tiles . . . painted and glazed in colours, namely blue, white, green and purple', commissioned in 1362 by Cardinal Audoin for his palace in Avignon from two potters from Manises, near Valencia, were probably of this type. The same is true of the large quantities of tiles ordered by King Peter IV of Aragón (r.1336–87) for the Royal Palace of Barcelona in 1367, and again for Tortosa Castle in 1370. Various archaeological finds in the Valencia region suggest that rectangular, hexagonal and diamond-shaped tiles were standard, though various more complex shapes were used to produce mosaic. At the Baños del Almirante (Baths of the Admiral), the remains of a pavement of white and green diamond-shaped tiles has been found, while at the baths of Torres Torres, green and white rectangular tiles were laid. Hexagonal purple tiles found at the late fourteenth-century Monastery of San Miguel de los Reyes must also have once been part of a floor.

In the production of *alicatados*, each piece of tile is glazed only one colour. This avoids the problem of separating different colours during firing. However, it demands much complex cutting of the tiles. The need to find faster and more economical means of production in order to satisfy increased demand therefore probably lay behind the adoption of the *cuerda seca* technique. Here, different coloured glazes are held apart by narrow, painted lines of manganese mixed with an oily substance which burns away in the kiln. Standard square and rectangular tiles could thus be made to reproduce the complex patterns achievable by panels of tile-mosaic. Though the technique had been used by the potters of Madinat al-Zahra' near

2.7 *Alizares* decorated using the *cuerda seca* technique, made in Toledo around 1500–50. Length 22.5cm and 23.3cm. V&A. 308:115&116-1866.

Córdoba in the mid-tenth century, and was practised at a range of sites across Spain in the eleventh century, it does not appear to have been applied to tile-making until the late twelfth or thirteenth century, and even then was not used widely until the fifteenth.

The earliest *cuerda seca* tiles were produced in Andalucía (fig. 2.5). These have become associated, perhaps erroneously, with Niebla, a regional capital prior to the reconquest. Whatever their exact origin, the 'Niebla' tiles are characterised by their particularly thick glazes, and were produced in a range of designs which incorporated the stars and interlacing lines also found on tile-mosaic. Later, in the second half of the fourteenth century, *cuerda seca* tiles were used to provide decoration in imitation of tile-mosaic above the arch of the Puerto del Vino at the Alhambra in Granada. By the fifteenth century, however, tile-makers in Seville were producing large quantities of standard *cuerda seca* tiles. These still routinely drew upon the established vocabulary of Moorish geometrical designs, despite the fact that an increasing number of the tile-makers were Christians and not *mudéjares* (or subject Muslims). By the start of the sixteenth century, other decorative influences were beginning to appear on the tiles (fig. 2.6). These included figurative and heraldic decoration in a Gothic idiom, but soon also Renaissance ornament. In addition, some tile designs were a hybrid of styles, combining some of the *mudéjar* elements with Renaissance foliage.

At the same time as these new styles were emerging, an important new production technique was developed that took the place of *cuerda seca*. This involved impressing the design into the tile with a mould, so as to leave raised lines between the areas to be glazed in different colours. Like *cuerda seca*, this new technique, termed *arista* or *cuenca*, also prevented colours from merging during firing. But because the use of moulds semi-mechanised the manufacturing process, levels of production could be increased. The use of relief decoration was not in itself new. From the thirteenth century, heraldic tiles with decoration in relief had been produced in Seville. And in the fourteenth century, relief-decorated tiles painted with coloured glazes on the raised areas appeared, for example, on another of the Alhambra gateways: the Puerta de la Justicia.

Once the problem of separating different glazes had been accomplished, and the form of tiles could be determined by function and practicality, a range of standard types emerged for different applications. In addition to the basic square and rectangular tiles used on floors and walls, tiles for more specific purposes were developed. Where two surfaces met at right angles, such as around wall recesses, on steps, or around altar frontals, *alizares* were used (fig. 2.7). These hollow oblong 'tiles' of square cross-section were made in the *cuerda seca* technique, or had painted decoration, as they were not robust enough to withstand the pressure required to impress a pattern in relief onto their two decorated surfaces. Ceiling tiles were made in a

Left: 2.8 Two *arista* ceiling tiles from the church of Santiago at Carmona, made in Seville around 1525–50. Rows of tiles would be fitted between the roof beams. Width 28.0cm. V&A. 97-1881.

Below left: 2.9 Small tiles known as *olambrillas* decorated stair risers or added colour to floors of plain tiles. The designs of these Toledan examples of around 1475–1500 were later copied by tile-makers in Seville. Each approx. 9.5cm sq. V&A. C.1192 & 1193-1919.

Above: 2.10 An *arista* tile depicting the arms of the Medici with the papal tiara and cross-keys, made in Seville by the workshop of Niculoso Francisco, around 1513–21. The tile is of the same type as those installed at the Castel Sant'Angelo in Rome. 13.5cm sq. V&A. 1108-1903.

2.11 *Arista* tiles decorated with interconnecting Renaissance-style urns in blue and lustre, made in Seville by the workshop of Niculoso Francisco, around 1500–30. Each 13.5cm sq. V&A. 982 to 984 & 986-1872.

variety of shapes and sizes, but a common type of *arista* ceiling tile was rectangular, with the complete design being formed across a pair of tiles (fig. 2.8). Mention should also be made of *olambrillas*, small decorated tiles which would be set among other plain or decorated tiles, or amid floors of red plaster (fig. 2.9).

Above all Spanish cities, Seville was the greatest producer of *cuerda seca* and *arista* tiles. A boom in the production of *cuerda seca* tiles around 1500 was quickly followed by the adoption of the *arista* technique, and vast quantities of such tiles were produced. Some of the earliest of these are associated with the great Italian potter Niculoso Francisco, who arrived in Seville shortly before 1500, and almost certainly played a part in the technique's development. Nothing is known with certainty of Niculoso's early life in Italy. He may have been trained in Florence, perhaps even in the workshop of Andrea della Robbia. However, by 1498 he appears to have been living in Triana, the principal pottery district of Seville. Niculoso's workshop produced large quantities of *arista* tiles, including those made for Pope Leo X for the Castel Sant'Angelo in Rome, some of which were decorated with emblems of the Medici family (fig. 2.10). He also received a commission to produce 6,000 *arista* tiles for the Sevillian monastery of San Pablo. In addition to his achievements with *arista* tiles, Niculoso is famed for having introduced painted tin-glazed tile pictures to Spain, and was probably also largely responsible for the introduction of Italian Renaissance ornament (fig. 2.11).

Another important tile workshop at this time was that of Juan Pulido, who, in 1538, along with his father Diego, produced the *arista* tiles for the spectacular Palace of the Marquise of Tarifa in Seville, now known as the Casa de Pilatos (fig. 2.12). Juan Pulido also produced tilework for the pavilion of Charles V, King of Spain (r.1516–56) and

Holy Roman Emperor (r.1530–56), in the gardens of the Real Alcázar (fig. 2.13). This included both *arista* tiles and *alicatados*, the latter forming the pavement and part of the walls. Panels of *alicatados* depicting the 'Pillars of Hercules', again made by Juan Pulido, were used in 1545 to decorate the Mexuar of the Alhambra, by then a palace of Charles V.

Seville's tile-makers also served a wide export market, assisted by the city's status as an important trading port. Their tiles can therefore be found in Italy, Portugal, the Low Countries and other sites throughout western Europe, as well as in South America. One of the most splendid monuments to Sevillian tilework is the Palace of Sintra in Portugal which was extensively tiled at the command of Manuel I (r.1495–1521) following a visit to Spain (fig. 2.14). Sevillian tiles also reached Britain, and a sizeable floor of *arista* tiles of around 1527 survives at the Lord Mayor's Chapel in Bristol.

While Seville was the largest production centre, and certainly responsible for the bulk of exports, other Spanish towns and cities produced *cuerda seca* and *arista* tiles. A strong tile-making tradition developed in Toledo, which probably began with the production of tile-mosaic, though none survives today. At the Aragonese town of Muel, a significant tile industry became established during the sixteenth century, with both *arista* and painted tiles being produced (fig. 2.15). However, the expulsion of the Moors from Spain in 1609 brought an end to the *mudéjar* tile-making traditions, though by this time they had largely been replaced by new styles and techniques.

Another branch of tile production to emerge in medieval Spain was that of painted tin-glazed earthenware tiles. The combination of painted decoration and tin glaze (lead glaze opacified by the addition of tin oxide) has provided ceramics with one of its greatest and most long-standing traditions, and one which by-and-large dominated the production of decorated tiles in Europe until the eighteenth century. Establishing an exact chronology for

Left: 2.12 The courtyard of the Casa de Pilatos in Seville, originally built around 1490 but extensively remodelled by Pedro Enríquez in 1520–39. The tiles were produced by the Pulido family around 1538.

Above: 2.13 The garden pavilion of Charles V in the gardens of the Real Alcázar in Seville.

the introduction and spread of the technique is problematic. Nevertheless, a broader picture of the shifting pattern of dominant trends and practices within the production and use of tiles can be observed.

The technique itself has its origins in the Near East, and was in use in Islamic Spain at the great pottery centre of Madinat al-Zahra' near Córdoba in the middle of the tenth century. Its earliest application to architectural ceramics appears to have been made later that century with the insertion of a narrow painted ceramic band set within the tessellated glass mosaic dome of the Mezquita in Córdoba.

However, painted tin-glazed floor tiles were first produced during the thirteenth century as part of the family of pottery decorated in green and purplish-black which extends from the Spanish provinces of Catalonia and Aragón, through southern France and into Italy. While it remains unclear where the first such tiles were made, their early distribution and subsequent development reflects the dominance of the medieval Kingdom of Aragón over the western Mediterranean. Not only did Aragón control most of Spain's eastern seaboard, but by 1283 it also ruled Sicily, and held a strong cultural influence over southern France. Production

2.14 Tiles specially made in Seville around 1500–10 for the Palace of Sintra. The armillary sphere depicted was a type of celestial globe used for navigation. Taken as an emblem by King Manuel I, it reflected Portugal's maritime prowess. 13.1cm & 15.0cm sq. V&A. 186-1853 & C.37-1973.

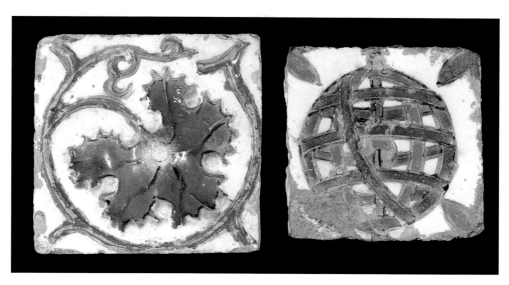

of green and purple tiles in Spain was carried out at Paterna near Valencia and Teruel in Aragón, as well as in Catalonia, where a floor of painted tiles was laid in the chapter house of Tarragona Cathedral before 1290. On the evidence of these and other related Catalonian tiles, naturalistic and fantastic animals were popular decorative motifs.

Another branch of painted tile production developed alongside the famous lustreware of Málaga and other sites in Andalucía. This technique, which used carefully controlled firing conditions to deposit thin films of metal from compounds painted onto the pottery, had been developed under the influence of potters from Egypt in the late twelfth century. With their gold-like sheen, the products were truly luxurious. The earliest known tiles decorated using the technique are those of the Cuarto Real de Santo Domingo in Granada, dating from the thirteenth century. Painted with arabesques in lustre alone, these specially shaped tiles form an upper border to the previously mentioned mosaic panels decorated with inscriptions. Large floor tiles bearing the Nasrid shield surrounded by finely painted arabesques in blue and lustre were made for the Alhambra during the fourteenth century (fig. 2.16). A curved section cut away from each of their corners allowed them to be laid in combination with small, circular tiles. During restorations to the Alhambra in the sixteenth century, the same designs were reproduced using the *arista* technique.

During the fourteenth century, the Valencia region became the principal lustreware production centre of Spain. Tile-making in the region had been dominated by the manufacture of monochrome-glazed tiles, but from the late fourteenth century and throughout the fifteenth, a flourishing tile industry ran alongside the production of lustre- and blue-painted pottery. Similar painted designs adorned both lustreware and tiles, and the same clays were used in their manufacture, although tiles were normally decorated in blue alone. In the production of most tin-glaze ceramics, an initial 'biscuit' firing of the unglazed items is followed by the application of the glaze and painted decoration, prior to a second 'glost' firing. However, the blue (cobalt oxide) decoration of the Valencian tiles was normally painted directly onto the unfired clay. After the first firing, the tile was glazed and fired again, the blue then emerging through the white tin glaze. Any lustre decoration would require an additional firing. Occasionally, painted decoration was used in conjunction with decoration in relief.

Tile production was carried out at Manises, Paterna and Gandía, and though there was a distinctive Valencian style, the products of the different centres are largely indistinguishable. Initially, the painted designs followed Islamic prototypes, and Martin I, King of Aragón (r.1395–1410) ordered tiles of this type for Barcelona Cathedral in 1402. However, the Gothic style was soon to become the dominant influence on the decoration of tiles. A wide range of designs became available, with different types of decoration being produced for different clients or sections of the market. Heraldic tiles were popular, and specific commissions were carried out for numerous wealthy Valencian families for whom such tiles acted as status symbols (fig. 2.17). Similarly, guilds, religious houses and civil institutions all commissioned tiles bearing their own emblems. Other tiles were produced in large quantities without any specific commission in mind. These

Above: 2.15 An *arista* tile panel depicting stylised flower vases and grotesque birds, made at Muel in Aragón, around 1550–1600. Width approx. 89.5cm. V&A. 605-1893.

Right: 2.16 A fourteenth-century tile from the Alhambra, painted in blue and lustre, and bearing an armorial shield adopted by the Nasrid sultans. Width 19cm. V&A. 382-1894.

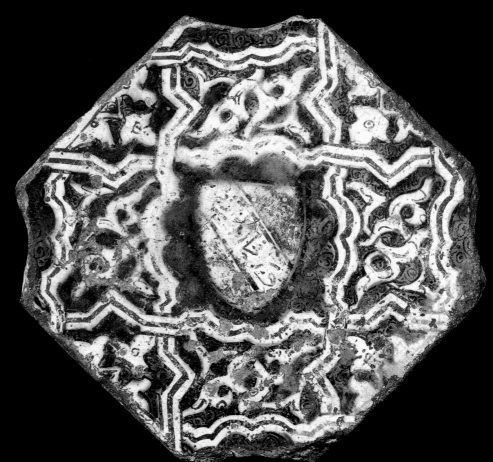

Right: 2.17 A ceiling tile from the castle of Conde de Parsent, made in Valencia around 1400–50. Width 41.8cm. V&A. 202-1881.

Above: 2.18 A group of tiles, including *alfardóns* with pious inscriptions, made in Valencia, probably at Manises, around 1400–50. The mottoes read: 'bon regiment' (a well-ordered life); 'ab sana pensa' (with right thoughts); 'ab saviesa' (with knowledge); 'ab diligencia' (with diligence). Total width approx. 30.5cm. V&A. 607A, 608A, 609, 610E-1893 & 6-1908.

were often decorated with Gothic flowers or foliage, or with animals, fantastic creatures, or knights and ladies. Another popular type of tile was decorated with pious religious inscriptions, often contained within a ribbon, and surrounded by delicate foliage (fig. 2.18). Most of the tiles were intended for use on floors, and a number of different shapes were employed. One especially popular type known as *alfardóns* were hexagonal with four short and two longer sides. Four of these tiles could be arranged around a square tile to form a regular octagon. Small, square *olambrillas* were also made for inserting into floors of plain, unglazed tiles (fig. 2.19). In an equivalent though more elaborate way, painted Valencian tiles of various polygonal shapes were set at regular intervals in the ceiling of the Convento

de la Concepción in Toledo in 1422. True ceiling tiles, or *socarrats*, were also produced. These were designed to fit between the roof-beams, and were made either using the tin-glaze technique or with decoration in red and black painted directly onto the clay and left unglazed (fig. 2.20).

Valencian tiles were exported throughout the western Mediterranean. They had reached the south of France by around 1425 where they satisfied a demand previously met by local products. In Italy, their popularity received a significant boost when Alfonso V, King of Aragón and Sicily (r.1416–58) and King of Naples from 1442, placed an order for tiles for Castel Nuovo in 1446. The commission was fulfilled by Juan Murcí, one of an especially notable family of Valencian tile-makers. Valencian tiles were also supplied for use in the Castel Sant'Angelo in Rome for Pope Nicholas V, around 1449, and again for the Appartamento Borgia of Pope Alexander VI, as late as 1494. The popularity of Valencian tiles in Catalonia led

another tile-maker, Pere Eiximeno, to go to Barcelona where he worked from 1452. By the end of the century a significant local production of blue-painted tiles had become established in Catalonia which, despite following Valencian prototypes, had its own distinguishing characteristics (fig. 2.21). The use of stencils lent the decoration a slightly stiff appearance, though this was to some extent offset by the practice of adding detail by scratching lines through the areas of blue-painted decoration (this technique being termed *sgraffito*). Production of blue and white tiles persisted throughout the sixteenth century in Catalonia, however in Valencia the industry declined early in the century, when the market became dominated by the *arista* tiles of Seville and Toledo.

In Italy, the technique of tin-glazing was known early in the thirteenth century, and production of tin-glazed pottery rapidly became established in central and southern regions. The earliest known tin-glazed tiles come from the high altar

Opposite left: 2.19 An *olambrilla*, made in Valencia around 1475–1500. The Gothic rose design was one of the most commonly used. 9.7cm sq. V&A. C.124-1932.

Opposite right: 2.20 Ceiling tiles from a house in Benaguacil, made either there or elsewhere in the Valencia region, around 1500–50. The tiles were painted in red onto a layer of slip, and left unglazed. Width of each approx. 30cm. V&A

Right: 2.21 Four tiles with painted and *sgraffito* decoration, made in Barcelona around 1550. Each 14.8cm sq. V&A. 1182 to C-1893.

of the basilica of St Francis at Assisi. Perhaps dating between 1236 and 1253, these tiles, painted with eight-pointed stars in green, brown and yellow, must have been set on the risers of the steps. Such a use seems to have been typical. Not unlike the pottery bowls which, like their counterparts in Aragón, had occasionally been cemented into the exterior walls of Italian churches of the twelfth and thirteenth centuries, tiles initially seem to have been used to provide accents of colour in architectural settings rather than to cover large surfaces. However, occasional examples of floors of glazed tiles are known from the thirteenth century, and floors of painted tin-glazed tiles make their first appearance at the end of that century at sites including the abbey church at Florence, the castle of Lagopesole, and the abbey of San Fructuoso di Camogli in Genoa.

In southern France, manufacture of tin-glazed painted floor tiles seems to have been practised at isolated sites from the middle of the thirteenth century. Though relatively scarce, these appear to have been the standard type of decorated tile in this part of France, where inlaid tiles are rare. Perhaps among the earliest examples are the tiles from the church of Saint-Julien at Brioude, painted with heraldic badges and stiff-leafed Gothic foliage (fig. 2.22). In Marseilles, a succession of workshops operated at Sainte-Barbe from the mid-thirteenth until the early fourteenth century. Tiles decorated with animals, heraldic emblems and foliate designs painted in green, brown and occasionally yellow, were produced there alongside tin-glazed pottery. In the south-west, painted tiles are known from the remote Cistercian abbey of Escaladieu in the foothills of the Pyrenees (fig. 2.23) and from several other sites in the region, including the abbey of Flaran. These were possibly all the products of a single workshop operating in the late thirteenth or early fourteenth century.

By the start of the fourteenth century, tin-glazed tiles of a high quality were being produced in the Avignon area. At

2.22 Part of a tile pavement from the collegiate church of Saint-Julien in Brioude, probably made around 1250–1300. Each approx. 12.1cm sq. V&A. 1551-1903.

that time, Avignon was an important international city and home to the papacy in exile from Rome. The potters of the region, working around Saint-Quentin-la-Poterie and Uzés, north-west of Avignon, and also in the lower Rhône valley, produced fine tin-glazed wares painted in green and brown as a luxury product. Some of these same potters also appear to have been responsible for the production of tiles, as the painted designs found on the pottery and tiles are closely related and both are made from fine white or pinkish clays, unlike the coarse red clays normally employed by French medieval tile-makers. Large quantities of tiles were ordered by the papal court from potters at Saint-Quentin-la-Poterie in 1317–19 and 1336, and tiles from this production centre have been found at the papal château at Châteauneuf-du-Papes and at a number of other sites, including the splendid Palais de Papes in Avignon. However, the majority of the tiles found at the Palais de Papes come from the lower Rhône area, where production appears to have begun at a slightly later date. A complete though badly worn floor made up of painted tin-glazed tiles set amid plain yellow and green lead-glazed tiles, survives *in situ* at the Palais de Papes in the *studium* of Pope Benoît XII. Tiles from the lower Rhône workshops have also been found at a number of other sites in the region, including the château de l'Empéri at Salon-de-Provence and the Palais des Archevêques in Narbonne.

Although at all these sites, painted tin-glazed tiles appear to have been the only decorated tiles used, they also appear in small numbers amid the pavements of inlaid and mosaic tiles produced by the itinerant Garonne valley workshop in the late thirteenth century. Of particular note are tiles including a finely painted male head in Gothic style from the Jacobins convent in Toulouse, and others decorated with figures and fantastical and naturalistic animals set within the splendid rectilinear mosaic floor of the chapel of Abbot Auger at the abbey of Lagrasse. The production of these finely painted tiles seems likely to have been aided by the proximity of artists and artisans working on the decorative schemes of these important building projects.

In the north of France, workshops producing painted tin-glazed tiles seem to have been extremely rare and confined to a very few areas. A small number of poorly made painted tiles dating from the early fourteenth century are known from the château-fort of Brain-sur-Allonnes in the Loire valley. More successful are the tiles made slightly later by a workshop in south-east Brittany, whose products are known from a number of sites including the ducal château of Suscinio. Here, around 1330–40, a splendid floor was laid which included four- and sixteen-tile groups painted with figures, animals and monsters in circular frames, set among mosaic panels and inlaid tiles. The painted tiles in these areas, like those of the Garonne valley workshop, formed only a small component of floors otherwise made up of lead-glazed tiles, although at Suscinio they were set in prominent positions.

Closely related to the painted tiles of the Loire valley and Brittany are others produced in Flanders and the Utrecht region around 1320–30, the technique perhaps having spread along with coastal trade. A number of sites with tin-glazed tiles are known in and around Utrecht, probably all the products of a single workshop. A monument to Pope Benedict V formerly in Hamburg Cathedral may also have been made by the Utrecht workshop, or a tile-maker from there. Of low rectangular form, the monument was covered with finely painted tin-glazed tiles, the only such tiles known in Germany. Upon the upper surface the Pope was shown beneath an architectural canopy. Around the edges of the monument were individual figurative tiles. Destroyed when the cathedral was demolished in 1806, the monument is known only through engravings and a few surviving fragments.

Numerous fourteenth-century tin-glazed tiles survive from sites in Flanders, including a virtually complete pavement from the Abbaye des Dunes which probably dates from the first half of the century. Production of painted tiles continued in Flanders throughout the fourteenth century. In 1364–6, 1,500 Flemish tiles were ordered by Edward III (r.1327–77) for Hadleigh Castle in

2.23 Two tiles from a chapel in the church of the Cistercian abbey of Escaladieu, dating from the late thirteenth or early fourteenth century. 11.4cm sq. and 12.1cm sq. V&A. C.962 & 963-1922.

Essex, and fragments of tin-glazed tiles from Flanders have been found there and elsewhere in Essex.

In the final decade of the century, under the patronage of Phillipe le Hardi, Duke of Burgundy, painted tiles were produced by Jehan le Voleur for the Duke's Flemish château at Hesdin. Le Voleur had initially worked at Ypres in conjunction with Jehan du Moustier. However, following difficulties in their working relationship, le Voleur established a separate workshop at Hesdin in 1391. Le Voleur, who later held the title of Painter to the Duke, was probably more involved with the design and painting of the tiles rather than their manufacture. The tiles seem to have been of excellent quality, and numerous floors were laid at Hesdin, with a further floor being laid at the Duke's residence in Arras in 1402. Unfortunately, none of these tiles are known to have survived.

Phillipe le Hardi and his brother, Jean de France, Duke of Berry, were also the patrons of an exceptional group of late fourteenth-century tin-glazed tiles. Unlike all the other medieval painted tiles of France, Flanders and the Netherlands, these tiles were painted in blue, and may even have incorporated lustre decoration. Both patrons employed Spanish tile-makers. Jehan de Gironne established a workshop in Dijon where he produced tiles for the Duke of Burgundy's oratory at the Chartreuse de Champmol between 1383 and 1388. Meanwhile, his compatriot Jehan de Valence, known as *le Sarrazin*, made tiles for the Duke of Berry's residences in Bourges and Mehun-sur-Yèvre before establishing a workshop at Poitiers in 1384 to make tiles for the Duke's palace.

Production of tin-glazed tiles in France and northern Europe appears to have almost entirely ceased during the fifteenth century, and any demand was met by imports from Spain and later Italy. It was not until the sixteenth century that the continuous production of painted tiles became established in the North, and then it was Italy rather than Spain that provided the major influence.

The Alhambra

The Alhambra, a fortified palatine city built on a hill overlooking Granada, is the supreme monument of the Nasrid kingdom. Though a castle had stood on the site from at least the ninth century, construction of the present Alhambra began at the command of the Sultan Muhammad I Ibn al-Ahmar in 1238, and was steadily developed throughout the thirteenth and fourteenth centuries.

Within the walls of the Alhambra are three distinct areas: the palace complex, the military Alcazaba, and the commercial and residential quarters which exclusively served the court. Of six Nasrid palaces that once stood within the Alhambra, only two

remain today. These, the Palacio de Comares and Palacio de los Leones, both date from the fourteenth century, and are extensively decorated with dazzling *alicatados*, whose intricate geometrical designs and myriad colours appear to dematerialise the walls, and combine with the ornate plasterwork above to create interiors of an extraordinary richness. Originally, pavements of *alicatados* or of lustre- and blue-painted tiles would also have been present, though virtually none of these have survived.

The unique identity of these palaces is today diminished, the two having been merged with the later Renaissance palace of

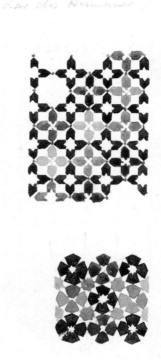

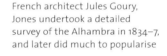

Opposite left: 2.24 The Patio de Comares, looking north towards the Torre de Comares in which was housed the sultan's private audience chamber, the Salón de los Embajadores. © Raghubir Singh.

Opposite top right: 2.25 Tile-mosaic from the Patio de Comares, dating from the second half of the fourteenth century. The panel demonstrates the ability of the tile-makers to cut complex, curved aliceres from fired ceramic slabs.

Opposite bottom right: 2.27 The Mirador de Lindaraja in the Palacio de los Leones. This intimate and richly decorated interior was likely a retreat of the sultan.

Above: 2.26 Drawings made by Owen Jones of tile-mosaic patterns in the Sala de los Dos Hermanas. Along with the French architect Jules Goury, Jones undertook a detailed survey of the Alhambra in 1834–7, and later did much to popularise Moorish design through the publication of *The Grammar of Ornament* and other works. V&A. 9156F.

Charles V. However their original characters were quite distinct. The Palacio de Comares, built under Isma'il I, Yusuf I, and completed by Muhammad V in 1370, was the official seat of the sovereign, and housed various judicial and administrative functions. The palace centred on the Patio de Comares, known also as the Patio de los Arrayanes (Court of the Myrtles), with its large rectangular pool, behind which lay the massive square tower housing the spectacular Salón de los Embajadores where the Sultan would receive important personages. Also adjacent to the courtyard lay the private apartments of the Sultan himself, and those of each of his four wives.

In contrast to the Palacio de Comares with its official and residential functions, the Palacio de los Leones was devoted to relaxation and entertainment. Probably completed around 1380, it was built in the form of an urban *villa*, with a colonnaded courtyard bounded by four reception halls. The tile-mosaic from the central Patio de los Leones has been completely lost, though it remains undisturbed in the Sala de los Dos Hermanas and in the intimate and sensuous Mirador de Lindaraja, where some of the most intricate and beautiful tilework can be found.

2.28 A doorway in the Patio del Cuarto Dorado of the Palacio de Comares. The patio acted as a courthouse. The richly ornamented wall in which the door is set was effectively the façade of the private palace, and formed the backdrop for the sultan's occasional presence when hearing a case in person.

RENAISSANCE AND MIGRATION

In Italy, the period from around 1440 to 1530 proved to be one of the most brilliant in the history of tiles. Not only was it a time of technical achievement, in which tile painters attained astonishing levels of subtlety and refinement, and exploited to the full the gradually increasing range of colours that were available, but it also saw the introduction of a new vocabulary of decorative motifs rediscovered from antiquity, and perhaps above all, witnessed a new level of unity in the conception of interior spaces that resulted in the closer integration of elements such as tiled floors within decorative schemes. By the start of the sixteenth century, the direct or indirect influence of Italian potters was to be felt at tile production centres throughout Europe.

The influence of Spain had been decisive in the development in Italy of painted tin-glazed (*maiolica*) floor tiles. Naples, which fell under Aragonese control in 1442, played a pivotal role in the spread of the practice. Large quantities of Valencian tiles reached Naples in this period, demand being fuelled by the prestigious commissions placed by Alfonso V for the Castel Nuovo, the Castello di Gaeta, and other new buildings of the Neapolitan court, made from 1446 onwards. Tiled floors following Valencian prototypes but using tiles of local manufacture appeared from the middle of the century. The earliest surviving example is that of the Carraciolo chapel in the church of San Giovanni a Carbonara at Naples, which dates from after 1442 and is composed of tiles probably made in the region (fig. 3.2). However, more than one workshop appears to have been involved in their production as the tiles exhibit technical as well as stylistic differences, and indeed may not all be of the same date. Some designs closely follow Valencian examples and may even have been imported, while others, such as a series of portraits, have a

strong Renaissance character. The pavement as it exists today could in fact incorporate tiles once laid in the nave of the church. Like the Carraciolo tiles, a number of later fifteenth-century pavements in Naples, such as that of the Brancacci chapel of Sant'Angelo a Nilo and the chapel of the Crocifisso dei Campanili at San Pietro a Maiella, follow the typical Spanish pattern of laying four elongated hexagonal tiles around each square tile. However, the finely painted tiles decorated with portraits and heraldry that once formed part of a pavement laid in the Duomo at nearby Capua around 1466–70 are of regular hexagonal form. Characteristic of all these later pavements is their extended palette, encompassing dark blue, green, yellow, brown and purple.

The arrangement of square and hexagonal tiles remained a standard model as the practice of laying pavements of tin-glazed tiles became established further north. The floor of the Mazzatosta chapel of Santa Maria della Verità in Viterbo, dating from around 1470, takes this form (fig. 3.3). A later example, from 1488, appears at the Bichi chapel of Sant'Agostino in Siena. Meanwhile, a pavement of around 1485 in the chapel of Basso della Rovere at Santa Maria del Popolo in Rome is composed of elongated hexagonal tiles only, all laid in the same orientation. But by this time, tile pavements which owed less to their Spanish predecessors had begun to appear. One such pavement was commissioned by Maria De Benedetti, abbess of the Convento di San Paolo in Parma from 1471–82. Its large

Right: 3.1 A panel depicting Susannah and the Elders, bearing the date 1565, set within ornamental tilework at the Quinta da Bacalhoa in Azeitão (see p67). Courtesy of Hirmer Verlag, Munich.

Above: 3.2 A tile from the church of San Giovanni a Carbonara in Naples, probably of local manufacture and dating from the mid-fifteenth century. Length 15.2cm. V&A. 1111-1903.

square tiles were boldly painted with figures and profile portraits of men and women in contemporary dress, animals and mythological subjects (fig. 3.4). The pavement was probably laid in a chapel in the gardens of the convent, though by the early nineteenth century the tiles had been removed and their arrangement is not recorded. The production of the San Paolo floor coincided with a period when the Italian *maiolica* potters had begun to compete successfully with imports of luxury Valencian pottery, and the production centres of north-central Italy, most notably Deruta, Montelupo, Faenza and Pesaro, attained dominance. The style of the decoration on the San Paolo tiles is closely related to the *maiolica* wares of Pesaro, and although their attribution is contested, it is from there that they probably came.

Most *maiolica* tiles of the period can in fact be related by their decoration to contemporary pottery. This is not surprising as tiles were generally made as special commissions by workshops producing a range of *maiolica* wares. However, the Florentine workshop of the Della Robbia family is something of an exception. Better known for their glazed terracotta reliefs, they produced floor tiles from around 1468. These were typically of large, regular hexagonal form, and decorated with simple floral designs (fig. 3.5). Often they were laid in imitation of carpets, even to the extent of adding painted 'fringes' on the border tiles that surrounded the central areas. Such tiles were laid in the chapel of Santa Fina at the collegiate church of San Gimignano in 1472–7, and in comparable floors in Empoli, near Florence, and Bologna. Around 1518, Luca della Robbia the Younger produced the elaborate tiled floor of Raphael's Loggia at the Vatican. This was almost certainly

made to a design by the artist himself, and sadly is today known only through drawings and a few surviving fragments.

As the fifteenth century began to draw to a close, the painted decoration on tiles tended to cover almost their entire surface, leaving virtually no undecorated white areas. Heralding this new fashion was the floor of the chapel of San Sebastiano dei Vaselli at San Petronio in Bologna. The main part of the pavement is composed of hexagonal tiles with stylised floral decoration and a series of portraits, including that of their painter, Pietro Andrea of Faenza. Rectangular border tiles meanwhile are decorated with Persian palmettes and foliage. Though bearing the date 1487 in commemoration of the concession of the chapel to Donato Vaselli, the floor is believed to have been made several years later. Following in this style in the sixteenth century, and perhaps also made in Faenza, were the tiles of the Lando chapel at San Sebastiano in Venice, dated 1510. Meanwhile, a group of tiles probably made in Pesaro have comparable decoration with those of the Lando chapel (fig. 3.6). These are known from several sites in Pesaro and nearby Fano, as well as the Casa di Francesco Cavazza in Saluzzo, where the tiles were installed only in the nineteenth century. One tile from the group bears the date '15011', presumably referring to either 1501 or 1511. The designs include a number of animals in landscapes set within roundels which prefigure those commonly found in the Netherlands in the next century.

Painted tin-glazed floor tiles in Renaissance Italy were typically used in relatively small-scale installations in prestigious locations, most frequently in private chapels dedicated to members of the

Left: 3.3 Tiles from the pavement laid in the Cappella Mazzatosta of the church of Santa Maria della Verità at Viterbo around 1470. V&A. 229-1902.

Above: 3.4 A tile from a pavement commissioned by Maria De Benedetti for the Convento di San Paolo in Parma, probably made in Pesaro between 1471 and 1482. Width 21.0cm. V&A. 12-1890.

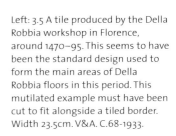

Left: 3.5 A tile produced by the Della Robbia workshop in Florence, around 1470–95. This seems to have been the standard design used to form the main areas of Della Robbia floors in this period. This mutilated example must have been cut to fit alongside a tiled border. Width 23.5cm. V&A. C.68-1933.

Above: 3.6 Unprovenanced tiles from a related group known from sites in Pesaro, where they were probably made around 1501–11. Each approx. 15cm sq. V&A. 333-1903.

Right: 3.7 Six tiles with emblems of the Gonzaga family, made at Pesaro in 1494, probably in the workshop of Antonio dei Fedeli. Each tile 23.5cm sq. V&A. 334-1903.

nobility as well as in their private apartments. Tiles were certainly an expensive and luxurious product, which, due to the vulnerability of the thin layer of tin glaze, were ill-suited to areas which received heavy wear. Their production was therefore dependent upon the availability of wealthy patrons.

The political map of northern Italy at the time was a complex one, composed of numerous self-governed cities and regions. Florence and Siena existed as independent republics, while other regions were ruled by seignorial families, such as the Gonzaga in Mantua and the Este in Ferrara and Modena. The patronage of such families came to be of great importance to artists and artisans, including potters. Floor tiles are known to have been commissioned by Duke Ercole I for the Villa di Schifanoia at Ferrara, though none survive. However, more is known of the tiles made for the Duke's daughter, Isabella d'Este, following her move to Mantua and marriage to Francesco Gonzaga. Thirteen cases of large floor tiles painted with a variety of emblems and mottoes of the Gonzaga family arrived at the Castello di San Giorgio on 1 June 1494 (fig. 3.7). Though intended for her husband's *camerino* at their villa at Marmirolo, some of the tiles were laid in Isabella's *studiolo* at San Giorgio, where they found favour both by virtue of their bold and colourful designs and their ability to deter mice. The tiles were most likely made in Pesaro, perhaps by Antonio dei Fedeli, who two years later wrote to Isabella d'Este concerning an order of tiles for which her agent had provided neither the payment nor the 'designi'. It therefore appears, as might be expected for such a commission, that the client was required to supply the pattern designs to the tile-maker.

Though the tiles in Isabella's *studiolo* at San Giorgio were clearly not conceived in relation to the room in which they were laid, to do so was seen as increasingly important.

By the sixteenth century it became standard architectural practice to use decoration to relate different planes of an interior space, and thus floor designs commonly reflect the structure of ceilings. This seems to have been true of a further set of octagonal tiles with mottoes of Isabella d'Este, the arrangement of which relates to the ceiling of her later *studiolo* in the Palazzo Ducale in Mantua, from where the floor perhaps came. However, the clearest example of such an interior, and one which epitomises the Renaissance fascination with classical architecture, can be found in the Santuario di Santa Caterina at the Oratario della Cucina in Siena. Here, the bosses and square compartments of the ceiling are mirrored directly by the structure of the floor, which is composed of square, circular and curved-ended rectangular tiles. Finely painted 'grotesques' cover the tiles, these being set against intensely coloured backgrounds. The earliest of the tiles date from 1504–9, but various additions and replacements have subsequently been made.

Closely related to the Cucina tiles are those from the palace of Pandolfo Petrucci in Siena, dating from around 1509 (fig. 3.8). In this floor, pentagonal tiles decorated with grotesques were set in a complex arrangement around square tiles bearing the arms of Piccolomini or Petrucci, or painted with figures in landscape settings. The walls of the palace were decorated with frescoes by Signorelli, Pintoricchio and probably also Giralomo Genga, and it is plausible that these artists had some influence on the designs used upon the tiles. This is true not only of the figures, but also of the tiles decorated with grotesques. Such decoration, typically composed of an elaborate curvilinear framework incorporating candelabra, trophies, monsters and the like, had become popular since the discovery in the late fifteenth century of the painted ornament of Nero's *Domus Aurea* in Rome, and had been

Opposite: 3.8 A section of the pavement of a principal room of the Petrucci Palace in Siena, made in Siena around 1509. Frescoes by Luca Signorelli and Pintoricchio which decorated the same room are now in the National Gallery in London. V&A. 4915 to 5386-1857.

Left: 3.9 Tiles from the Petrucci Palace in Siena, probably produced as part of the restoration to the pavement carried out by Giralomo di Marco of Siena around 1600. Width approx. 26.7cm. V&A. 966B, 967, 969, 976 & 977-1892.

Below: 3.10 A tile from the Rocca Paolina in Perugia, possibly made by the workshop of Francesco Durantino in Perugia in the mid-sixteenth century. Height 18.4cm. V&A. 441-1906.

used to great effect by Pintoricchio in the decoration of the Piccolomini Library in Siena Cathedral around 1507. Interestingly, the library was also paved with painted tiles at this time, though these bore a simple design of a crescent from the Piccolomini arms upon tiles of triangular form. Grotesque ornament, which was to become a principal feature of mannerist design, endlessly transmitted and modified throughout Europe, was further popularised by Raphael's decoration for his Vatican Loggia. This scheme, with its sinuous decoration on a white ground, was copied widely, and by the later sixteenth century, *maiolica* with white-ground grotesque decoration was produced in huge quantities. Such designs were used on a later set of tiles from the Petrucci Palace, these probably having been made for restorations to the original pavement carried out by Giralomo di Marco of Siena around 1600 (fig. 3.9).

Among sixteenth-century pavements exhibiting the virtuosity characteristic of mannerist design, a series of tiles from the Rocca Paolina in Perugia is exceptional. This

massive fortress was built by the decree of Pope Paul III and officially completed in 1543. Payments for paving tiles ordered from a number of different production centres are recorded by 1545. Of particular interest, however, are the surviving fragments of a floor, seemingly of circular form, incorporating balustraded friezes of trophies and grotesque ornament set against an intense blue ground (fig. 3.10). The style of the decoration suggests a connection with the production centre of Castel Durante (now Urbania). A likely hypothesis is that the tiles were produced by Francesco Durantino, a *maiolica* painter from that town who from 1547 worked at a kiln at Monte Bagnola in Perugia.

The painterly brilliance of the original Petrucci Palace tiles is matched by those of a near-contemporary pavement in a chapel commissioned by the physician Bartolomeo Lombardini, in the church of San Francesco at Forlì (fig. 3.11). Following Lombardini's death in 1512, the chapel was apparently completed by his daughter Joanna and her husband Giovanni Monsignani, and their arms appear on tiles from the pavement. Also present among the set is a tile signed 'Petrus' and dated 1513, while another is dated 1523. The arrangement again is a complex one, with various polygonal tiles set around a series of central octagonal tiles. This central series, with its delicately drawn portraits of musicians, artists, and even the tile painter himself, seems to reflect the humanist concerns of the Renaissance. Other of the octagonal tiles show classical heads or creatures from mythology, again exemplifying the interests of the time. Meanwhile, the tiles filling the interstices are decorated with delicate arabesques in blue, far from the heavy tonality of the Petrucci floor. The tiles were probably made at Forlì, or possibly in Faenza.

In Deruta, a locally made floor, dated 1524, was laid in a chapel of the church of Sant'Angelo. This had been commissioned by the Compagnia del Rosario, which had its seat in the church, but when this was transferred to the church of San Francesco the pavement was likewise moved. The floor is unusual in its composition of star and pointed cross-shaped tiles, a form primarily associated with Islamic tilework and in particular that of Iran. The crosses are decorated with stylised foliage and delicate arabesques on a blue ground, while the stars carry a series of figurative designs of considerable refinement, drawing upon a wide range of printed sources (fig. 3.12). Among these are

3.11 Part of the tile pavement of the Lombardini chapel in the church of San Francesco at Forlì, probably made locally, around 1513–23. The church was demolished around 1800, the tiles reputedly being relaid in a private villa. The V&A acquired the pavement almost in its entirety in 1866. V&A. 30-1866.

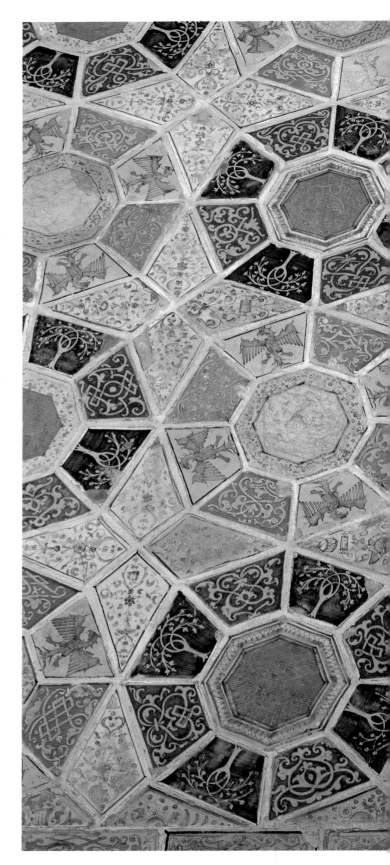

examples of the work of an accomplished *maiolica* painter whose hand has been recognised in a number of finely painted *maiolica* dishes. The workshop which produced the pavement nevertheless remains unknown. Certain later sixteenth-century pavements from Deruta, however, appear to be the products of the workshop of Giacomo Mancini (known as 'El Frate'). An example, dated 1566, can be found in the church of Santa Maria Maggiore in Spello. Arabesques on a blue ground again appear, though here they provide decorative borders for panels of polychrome grotesque ornament.

Not all the *maiolica* floors of Renaissance Italy were so ornately decorated. Although they were essentially reserved for prestigious locations rather than basic functional floors, pavements of plain *maiolica* tiles are known. One favoured arrangement seems to have been a chequerboard pattern of alternating blue and white tiles, and such a floor was laid in

the Cappella Barozzi in the Vescovado at Padua around 1491. It was probably for pavements of this type that 5,000 blue and white tiles were ordered on behalf of the Duke of Urbino from a group of Urbino potters in 1523. This commission, which came about in the most casual way when Giralomo Genga, the Duke's artist and architect, met the potters by chance on the road back to Urbino, had previously been rejected by potters from Pesaro for offering too little profit.

During the sixteenth century, Castelli in the Abruzzo region emerged as a major *maiolica* production centre, and here notable tiles were produced. Floor tiles finely painted with arabesques in white on a tin glaze coloured a deep blue through the addition of cobalt followed more standard polychrome types in the second half of the century. Ceiling tiles were also made for the nearby church of San Donato (fig. 3.13). Decorated with portraits, foliate motifs and inscriptions, these were close in style to the so-called Orsini-Colonna wares produced in Castelli. Later, in 1615–17, the church was rebuilt and the ceiling fitted with a splendid new series of tiles decorated with similar motifs but in the new and less crowded *compendiario* style. This remarkable ceiling, which appears to have been the result of a collaboration between many local potters, has survived largely intact.

From the late fifteenth century, the movement of Italian potters to other parts of Europe resulted in the dramatic dissemination of their styles and techniques. Even as early as 1470–80, a *maiolica* workshop producing tiles and other wares was in operation at Buda Castle in Hungary, presumably established by Italian potters brought to the palace at the behest of the King, Matthias Corvinus (r.1458–90). By the end of the century, Niculoso Francisco

Above: 3.12 A tile from a pavement dated 1524, originally laid in a chapel of the church of Sant'Angelo in Deruta, then removed to the church of San Francesco and now largely in the Museo Civico di Deruta. Width 20.3cm. V&A. C.257-1909.

Right: 3.13 A ceiling tile from Castelli, probably made in the workshop of the Pompei family in the mid-sixteenth century. The tile is one of a series which adorned the church of San Donato near Castelli. Width 25.4cm. V&A. C.306-1927.

3.14 The pavement in the chapel of The Vyne in Hampshire. The tiles were probably produced by the workshop of Guido Andries and may originally have been laid around 1522. National Trust Photographic Library. Photographer: Angelo Hornak.

was in Seville, and early in the sixteenth century other Italian potters were at work in Lyon in France as well as in Antwerp, then a thriving city of the Spanish Netherlands. A significant Italian mercantile community had become established in Antwerp by this time, and it is certain that the city's authorities would have looked favourably upon the introduction of the new industry. By 1513, at least three Italian *maiolica* potters were at work there, as a trial records their names: Janne Maria de Capua, Jan Francisco de Bresse and Guido [di Savino]. Janne Maria was recalled to Italy soon afterwards by the Duke of Milan. However, Jan Francisco, who became known as Jan Frans, and Guido di Savino, who adopted the name Andries, were to remain in the city.

Andries was born in Castel Durante and had worked in Venice prior to his arrival in Antwerp sometime before 1508. From 1520 he lived and worked in a house called *Den*

Salm (The Salmon) in Cammerstraat. This was to become the most celebrated of Antwerp's *maiolica* workshops, and attracted prestigious patrons both at home and abroad. The famous tiles of the chapel at The Vyne in Hampshire may well have been produced there (figs 3.14 and 3.15). They represent the typical sixteenth-century Antwerp *maiolica* pavement, with square tiles bearing portraits and animals being enclosed by hexagonal tiles decorated with Persian palmettes and other foliate designs reminiscent of the border tiles of the Vaselli chapel. The tiles may have been bought for the house by Sir William Sandys on a visit to Antwerp, and laid around 1522. The arrangement of the pavement is not, however, original, the tiles reputedly having been rediscovered in a heap in the garden during the nineteenth century.

Floors like that of The Vyne seem to have been highly fashionable in England in the early sixteenth century. Similar tiles have been found at a number of royal, monastic and

3.15 Large square tiles decorated with portraits and other designs at The Vyne. Each approx. 19.5cm sq. National Trust Photographic Library. Photographer: John Bethell.

mercantile sites in London and the south-east, including Cardinal Wolsey's manor The More in Hertfordshire, the Tower of London, and Whitehall Palace. Andries himself is even recorded as having been offered 'good wages and howserowm' by Henry VIII in order that he should practise his art in England, though this came to nothing. He did, however, produce a floor for Philip of Burgundy,

Bishop of Utrecht, in 1524, and may well have been responsible for the most complete surviving pavement of its type, that of the choir of the abbey of Herkenrode, now in the collections of the Musées Royaux d'Art et d'Histoire in Brussels. This pavement, similar in decoration to that of The Vyne, had been ordered by Abbess Mathilde de Lexhy in 1532 and was to be installed by Easter Day the following

Right: 3.16 A floor tile bearing the arms of Bacon and Whaplode, thought to have come from Gorhambury, Sir Nicholas Bacon's house in Hertfordshire. Such tiles may have been among the products of Andries and Jansen while in Norwich. 13.4cm sq. V&A. 4603-1863.

Far right: 3.17 A floor tile depicting a turtle, probably made in Aldgate around 1600–15. 13.4cm sq. V&A. C.144-1991.

year. Though the order was placed with Jan Frans' brother, Peter, he must have acted as a middle-man as he was not himself a potter. Comparable tiles, also perhaps products of Andries' workshop, are known from the sanctuary of the abbey of Hemiksem, and other sites in Belgium.

After Guido Andries' death sometime before 1541, his widow married Jan Frans' nephew Franchois, who ran *Den Salm* until 1562. It was then bought by Guido's son Lucas, who had been running his own workshop, *De Goudbloem*, in the Steenhouwersvest, since 1556. Four of Guido's other sons also became potters. Guido II Andries ran two workshops in Antwerp, the first at the Ouver, and then from 1577 to 1615, *De Tennen Pot* in Sint-Jansvliet, which he ran with Andries Eynhouts. Joris Andries had a small workshop opposite *Den Salm*. Meanwhile, Frans Andries went to Seville, and Jasper Andries to Norwich. Though the Andries family dominated *maiolica* production in Antwerp, there were many other workshops at the time. The Italian influence was nevertheless strong. Both the type of kilns used and the manufacturing technologies employed owed much to Italy, and were close to those described in Cipriano Piccolpasso's famous treatise on *maiolica* production, written in the mid-sixteenth century. Meanwhile, excavations of kiln waste at *De Goudbloem* and a site in the Shoysterstraat have given an indication of the relative scale of production of different object types. In these cases, over three-quarters of the pottery produced was made up of standard dishes and plates. Tiles accounted for around one-tenth of the output, the rest being pharmacy jars and small quantities of jugs and bowls.

Not all floor tiles made in Flanders were of the Herkenrode type. A pavement in the chapel of the château de Rameyen, produced sometime between 1527 and 1549, is decorated with grotesques copied from Italian engravings. And as well as floor tiles, pictorial tile panels were produced in Antwerp from the 1540s. The splendid panel depicting the *Conversion of St Paul* in the Vleeshuis Museum in Antwerp, along with a number of other fragmentary panels, can be attributed to the *Den Salm* workshop. Such panels are likely to have been made under the influence of Spain where the practice was first introduced. The skill and expertise of the Antwerp potters is also proven by the production of a more unusual product, that of tin-glazed stove tiles. Fragments from a stove dating from the first quarter of the sixteenth century from the site of the abbey of St Mary Graces in London represent the earliest known tin-glazed stove tiles in north-west Europe. Analysis of these has proved they were made in Antwerp. Prior to the sixteenth century, examples of tin-glazed stove tiles are known only from isolated sites in central Europe, the technique perhaps reaching Austria from Hungary, where stove tiles were among the products of the kilns at Buda castle. Painted tin-glazed decoration was, however, to become the dominant technique employed by stove-tile-makers in Alpine Europe, and was famously practised by the workshop of Ludwig Pfau at Winterthur in Switzerland from around 1575.

For much of the sixteenth century, the seventeen provinces of the Netherlands, which included what is now Belgium and Luxembourg, were united under the control of Spain. However, the uprising of 1566 began a period of unrest, fuelled in part by Catholic and Protestant divisions, which resulted in the independence of the predominantly Protestant northern provinces in 1585. This period of disquiet and religious intolerance, and in particular the sacking of Antwerp by the Spanish in 1576, prompted many

3.18 Reproductions of the tiles from the monastery church of Brou, made in the late nineteenth century by Leon Parvillée for use at the Château de Chenonceau. Parvillée's copies provide a measure of the richness of the original floor. V&A. 333-1895.

of the population, potters among them, to leave for the northern provinces. Joris Andries settled in Middleburg in 1564, while Adriaen Boegart established one of the three *maiolica* workshops known to have been in operation in Haarlem in 1568. Others followed, and during the last quarter of the century the production centres of the northern provinces of the Netherlands attained dominance over Antwerp. The process by which this occurred was, however, more gradual than has sometimes been imagined.

Maiolica workshops had in fact already been established in Utrecht and Bergen op Zoom during the first half of the century, though their production must have been small. And in Antwerp, where a partial renewal of the industry followed the 1585 partition, production continued until at least 1627, when Adriaen van Hauten was recorded to be making tiles, pharmacy jars and plates at his pottery in the Shoystestraat. Indeed, there is evidence that workshops in the north and south produced comparable products in this period. Tiles decorated with animals and flower vases in lozenges, a standard type normally associated with the northern Netherlands (fig. 4.5), have also been found at the site of Guido II Andries' *De Tennen Pot* workshop in Antwerp.

Antwerp *maiolica* potters also travelled to England. In 1570, Jasper Andries and Jacob Jansen famously petitioned Queen Elizabeth I for the exclusive rights to practise their craft, and sought a riverside site in London for their workshop. In the petition they stated that they had come to England three years earlier to avoid persecution, since when they had been 'exercising the makinge of Galley pavinge tyles' – in other words, tin-glazed floor tiles – as well as pharmacy jars and other wares. This must have been at Norwich, where Jasper's brother Joris also appeared in 1567 before returning to Middleburg (fig. 3.16). Although the petition to Queen Elizabeth was unsuccessful, Jansen went on to establish a pottery at Aldgate in London in 1571, where he was assisted by six other Flemish potters. The Aldgate pottery continued after Jansen's death in 1592, surviving until about 1615, around which time two other potteries producing tin-glazed earthenware became established across the Thames at Southwark (fig. 3.17). Jasper Andries, on the other hand, took up residence in Colchester, where he was joined by his brother Lucas.

In southern France, the occasional examples of tin-glazed floor tiles made in the late fifteenth century betray a strong Spanish influence. A group of tiles with simple foliate designs in blue and white are known from sites in the Avignon area. Though directly based on Spanish prototypes they may have been made locally. Similarly, a floor of square and hexagonal tiles from the Château de Combefa near Albi in south-west France resembles Valencian products and could have been made in France by Spanish craftsmen. However, the tiles made in 1495 for the Château de Longecourt-en-Plaine in Cote d'Or show new decorative influences. Two groups of tiles from the château are known. The first combine simple line-impressed decoration with a white tin glaze and areas painted in blue. The second comprises a series of portraits, landscapes, heraldic motifs and mottoes, suggesting an Italian influence. Also startling is the polychrome palette of blue, purple, yellow and green.

In the Île-de-France, where painted tile pavements were unknown in the Middle Ages, *maiolica* floor tiles made their appearance under the patronage of the King, François I (r.1515–47). The Florentine ceramicist Giralomo della Robbia, who produced architectural *faïence* for the Château de Madrid in the Bois de Boulogne around 1527, may also have been responsible for the colourful floor tiles

3.19 An heraldic panel bearing the arms of Anne de Montmorency impaling those of his wife Madeleine de Savoie, from the pavements laid in the Château d'Ecouen in 1542, produced by the workshop of Masseot Abaquesne in Rouen. Width approx. 66cm. V&A. 8491-1863.

painted with foliate decoration which came from the château. Fragments of painted tiles found at the Palais de Louvre suggest that François I may also have ordered tiles for some of the rooms of the old palace at around the same time. These appear to be the only instances of royal commissions for painted tiles in sixteenth-century France, though such tiles continued to make spectacular if occasional appearances in other prestigious buildings during the course of the century.

The tile pavements of the monastery of Brou, near Bourg-en-Bresse, were noted for their brilliance. A sixteenth-century account by Guillame Paradin described them as being as 'delightful to see as it is possible to find', but by the end of the seventeenth century the tiles were already much worn (fig. 3.18). The principal pavement from Brou is composed of square portrait tiles surrounded by elongated hexagonal tiles painted with branches which frame the portraits. Two further pavements from Brou were made up of square tiles, one decorated with branches, the other with medallions containing classically inspired candelabra and acanthus foliage. The original locations of

Left: 3.20 A section of a pavement from the Château d'Ecouen, produced by the workshop of Masseot Abaquesne in Rouen around 1550. The complete border of blue tiles around the panel is misleading. As originally laid, the floor was composed of a series of interlinked circles and squares bearing heraldic emblems. V&A. 8533-1863.

Right: 3.21 A watercolour plan of the pavement of the Chapelle Saint-Croix at Langres Cathedral, as prepared by Léon Parvillée during his restoration work of 1880–4. V&A. 65-1893.

these two pavements remain unclear, though the main pavement was laid in the choir of the church and in the chapel of Marguerite d'Autriche, and must date from 1531–2. No contemporary documentary evidence has yet been found to establish where the tiles were made or by who. However, a seventeenth-century account claims they 'were made by one François de Canarin in one of these forests'. Scientific analysis has indeed shown the clays used to be local, though whether the potters involved were Italian, Flemish, or in some way connected with the *maiolica* workshops established in Lyon, remains unclear. The techniques used in the production of the tiles are, in fact, unusual. The tiles are very thick and formed from a coarse red-firing clay more typical of lead-glazed floor tile production. To this, a coating of white slip was applied before glazing and painting the tiles.

The most celebrated painted tin-glazed (*faïence*) tiles in Renaissance France are those from the Château d'Ecouen. The château was rebuilt to an austere and modern design for one of the country's richest noblemen, Anne de Montmorency, following his appointment as Constable of France, and made more comprehensive use of painted tilework than any other French building of the period. Montmorency, who had previously ordered tiles from Antwerp for the Château de Fère-en-Tardenois, this time turned to Masseot Abaquesne, a potter from Rouen. The first series of tiles was made for the château in 1542 (fig. 3.19). These formed pavements bearing the arms of Anne de Montmorency and his wife Madeleine de Savoie, and seem to have been laid in a gallery in the west wing of the château as well as in their private apartments and perhaps also the chapel, where similar emblems appear on the ceiling. The floors were composed of a series of square compartments, each containing a coat of arms painted across a set of sixteen tiles and surrounded by a border of blue tiles. Each square compartment was then divided from the next by a single row of tiles bearing fruit and vegetable motifs, with a further border of blue tiles being laid around the edges of the room. In the same year, Abaquesne also produced a series of pictorial panels depicting scenes from Roman history, though it is not clear where in the château these were sited.

AVTEL

On the occasion of the accession of Henri II (r.1547–59), a frequent visitor to Écouen, new decorations to the château were ordered, and Abaquesne was commissioned to produce a new pavement (fig. 3.20). This consisted of a series of heraldic emblems held within square or circular blue frames which were linked by smaller circular frames containing the monogram of Montmorency and his wife. The primary heraldic emblems were divided so that on one row were the arms of Montmorency, his wife, and his badge of office, while on the next were the arms of Henri II and Catherine of Medici. The white ground between the various heraldic motifs was covered with finely drawn grotesques borrowed from Jacques Androuet Du Cerceau. The pavement was made around 1550, probably at the same time as a further series of pictorial panels depicting The Flood, which were perhaps installed in the chapel or sacristy. Following his work at Écouen, Abaquesne went on to produce tiles for Claude d'Urfé, the governor of Henri II's children. The pavement he made for the Château de la Bâtie d'Urfé, dated 1557, is closely related in style to his work at Écouen, and carries the emblems of d'Urfé and his wife Jeanne de Balsac.

Two further splendid French *faïence* pavements of the mid-sixteenth century were those of the Château de Polisy and Langres Cathedral. It is possible that they were products of the same workshop, though they are no longer believed to be the work of Abaquesne, as has been thought in the past. The boldly painted pavement at Polisy, bearing various Renaissance ornament and allegorical figures contained within a framework of octagons and Greek crosses, bore the dates 1545 and 1549, that is, shortly after the château was rebuilt for the Dinteville family. The pavement was installed in a first-floor room, quite probably the one in which was hung Hans Holbein's famous painting 'The Ambassadors', which depicts John de Dinteville and his friend Georges de Selve in 1533. The design of the pavement, which is similar to that of carved wooden ceilings of the period, was copied from a design published by the influential Italian architect Sebastiano Serlio in 1537. In true Renaissance fashion, the colourful pavement of the Chapelle Saint-Croix at Langres Cathedral directly reflects the design of its own vaulted ceiling (fig. 3.21). The tiles were laid in 1551, soon after the new chapel was added to the medieval cathedral. Extensive restoration of the floor was undertaken by Léon Parvillée between 1880–4.

Until the middle of the sixteenth century, the production of *faïence* in France had been restricted to a number of prestigious sites and small, isolated workshops. However, the arrival of Italian potters in Nevers from around 1580, including some who had previously worked in Lyon, not only established the town as an important production centre but marked the start of a period of expansion and increasing industrialisation. One alliance between Italian potters at Nevers was made at the command of Louis de Gonzague, a member of the famous Mantuan family, who had gained the title of Duc de Nevers on his marriage to Henriette de Clèves. This alliance was made between Augustin Conrade, a potter from Albisola near Savona who had arrived in Nevers in 1584, and Jules Gambin, a *maiolica* painter from Faenza who had previously worked in Lyon. It is likely that Louis brought the potters together in order for them to produce the floor tiles for the Ducal palace at Nevers. A number of tiles from the palace, painted with Gonzaga emblems and Italianate foliage, are conserved in the Musée Frederic Blandin in Nevers. Variants of these tiles with different border patterns may have been made slightly later, perhaps for Louis' son Charles I. Another member of the Conrade family, the celebrated potter Antoine Conrade, also became involved in the production of painted tin-glazed floor tiles. In 1636, he received an order for 480 tiles for Marie de la Tour, Duchesse de la Trémouille. These tiles, destined for the Château de Thouars in Deux-Sèvres, were to be painted with the arms of the Duchess, according to a design which accompanied the order.

One earlier commission of tin-glazed floor tiles for a prestigious client is deserved of mention. Between 1611 and 1618, a series of painted *maiolica* pavements made in Montelupo were sent as diplomatic gifts from the Grand Duke Cosimo II of Tuscany to Maria de Medici in Paris, and in these the Queen apparently took great delight. Nevertheless, by the mid-seventeenth century the era of pavements of painted tin-glazed tiles being laid as symbols of power and prestige had begun to draw to its close in France, and both the availability of painted tiles, and the uses to which they were put, were set to change.

Tile-making in Spain was also much influenced by Italian and Flemish potters during the course of the sixteenth century. This was particularly true in Seville and Talavera. The Italian Niculoso Francisco, as we have seen, played an important role in the development and production of *arista* tiles following his arrival in Seville at the end of the fifteenth century. However, he also made painted tin-glazed tiles. Though similar to Italian *maiolica* tiles in terms of their technique and palette, Niculoso took the novel step of producing tile pictures, in which large compositions were painted across whole panels of tiles. His first known work of this type was the tomb of Iñigo López in the church of

Santa Ana in Triana, Seville, from 1503. This pictorial representation of an effigy was originally sited on the floor of the church, but has since been moved to a wall. The following year Niculoso produced the tilework for the Altar of the Visitation in the Real Alcázar, which includes panels depicting the Visitation, the Tree of Jesse and the Annunciation, amid a framework of Renaissance ornament. The designs for the main panels perhaps derive from a Flemish or German Book of Hours, while the grotesques are probably taken from engravings brought by the potter from Italy. Similar grotesques appear on the tilework of the monumental doorway of the Convento de Santa Paula in Seville, which Niculoso carried out in the same year (fig. 3.22). However, his greatest undertaking was perhaps the tiled altarpiece of the monastery of Tentudía in Badajoz of 1518.

A few painted tiles may have been made by Niculoso's son, Juan Battista, following his father's death around 1529. Otherwise, there was a hiatus in their production in Seville until the arrival from Antwerp of Frans Andries, the son of Guido di Savino. Andries signed a contract in 1561 in which he agreed to teach the Sevillian potter Roque Hernández the art of making painted tiles and *maiolica*. No known tiles can be attributed with certainty to either Andries or Hernández, but those of Cristóbal de Augusta, Hernández's son-in-law, are celebrated. His most extensive commission was to produce tiles for the Salón de Baile at the Real Alcázar, completed in 1577–9 (fig. 3.23). The high tiled wainscots that surround the halls are boldly painted on a striking yellow ground with strapwork and ornament deriving from Italian and Flemish sources. Among other dated works is the Virgin of Rosary panel of 1577, now in Seville's Museo de Bellas Artes. Following in the tradition of Augusta, the Valladares family dominated the market for painted tiles in Seville in the first half of the seventeenth century. They too produced grand schemes, providing tiles for wainscots, altar-frontals and floors, all boldly painted in

3.22 The doorway of the Convento de Santa Paula in Seville, with tiles made by Niculoso Francisco in 1504. The ceramic roundels and sculptural decorations were also probably produced in Niculoso's workshops, assisted by the sculptor Pedro Millán whose signature one roundel bears.

a rich polychrome palette. The wainscots of the Convento de Santa Paula, of 1617–31, provide one example among many in Seville, their work also being found at sites throughout Andalusía, Portugal and South America. Meanwhile, a small garden room at the Real Alcázar provides a rare surviving example of a Valladares floor, albeit in extremely worn condition.

A similarly rich heritage of painted tilework developed in Talavera in central Spain following the arrival of the Flemish potter Jan Floris. Earlier, around 1551, Floris had established a workshop in Plasencia, from where he supplied figurative and armorial tile panels to churches there and in Cáceres, and also seems to have provided the tiles for the floors of both the church of Santa María in Medina de Rioseco and the palace of Licenciado Butrón at Valladolid. However, in 1562, Floris was summoned by Philip II (r.1556–98) and ordered to move his workshop to Talavera. Here he was to produce tiles for the Alcázar in Madrid, and for the King's hunting lodges of El Pardo and Valsaín. Though nothing remains of these buildings or their tiles, it is likely that the tilework was extensive and included large pictorial panels. Nevertheless, from those of his tiles which are known, it is clear that he was responsible for the introduction of Renaissance ornament into the pottery of the region, and in particular for the adoption of the strapwork motifs evolved by the Flemish engravers Cornelis Bos and Cornelis Floris, the potter's brother.

Floris died in 1567, and for a time Juan Fernández, perhaps a pupil of Floris, received royal patronage. From 1570, Fernández supplied tiles for the monastery of Escorial, though later lost the commission to Jusepe de Oliva, a tile-maker from Toledo. Nevertheless, tile production in Talavera had become firmly established by this time. A report for Philip II of 1575 praised Talaveran tiles for their quality and noted their export to Portugal and the Indies. A record made in 1596 by Friar Andrés de Torrejón tells of how over 200 people worked every day in the town's eight potteries, and records how the tiles were used to decorate altar-frontals, temples, gardens, salons and dining rooms. Interestingly, he calls the tiles used for altar-frontals 'as attractive as silk', an apt description in that the designs of these panels were at times made in imitation of embroidery. The names of numerous Talaveran tile-makers are recorded in documents of the period, though it is frequently difficult to relate these to existing panels of tiles. Antonio Díaz may have been responsible for the tiles in the Toledan churches of Erustes, Nombela, and Domingo Pérez, the first two of which are dated 1567. The panels now assembled in the portico of the church of Nuestra Señora del Prado in Talavera were probably made locally, though the individual potters are not known. The same is also true of the splendid series of pictorial panels depicting The Life of the Virgin commissioned specifically for the same church in 1638. Among other notable Talavera commissions, Fernando de Loaisa carried out work for the palace of the Duque del Infantado in Guadalajara in 1595, though these panels were destroyed in the Spanish Civil War.

The production of painted tiles also became established in Toledo in the middle of the sixteenth century. Jusepe de Oliva, who had won the Escorial commission from Fernández in 1577, was perhaps the most notable of the Toledan tile-makers. In 1575 he produced tiles decorated with acanthus foliage for the octagonal floor of the chapel of the de la Cerda Palace in Toledo, and was also responsible for the pictorial panels depicting The Three Estates from the Generalitat in Valencia. From 1578, perhaps the year of Oliva's death, a number of other Toledo potters, including Juan de Vera, received large royal commissions for tiles and garden pottery, and it is clear that the scale of production was sizeable. Elsewhere in Spain, in Valencia and Catalonia, potters were slower to respond to the new styles and polychrome palette imported by Italian and Flemish potters, and tiles of traditional types painted in monochrome blue or blue and lustre continued to be made. However, by the last decades of the sixteenth century, tiles with Italianate ornament began to be produced, and the Sevillian and Talaveran fashions for tiling walls and altar-frontals also became popular.

In Genoa and Sicily, Spanish tile-making had a marked influence. During the medieval period and the Renaissance, Genoa was a major maritime power with close links to Spain. The production of *maiolica* tiles, initially made in imitation of imports from Valencia, became firmly established in the region during the fifteenth century. In 1485, the workshop of Giovanni Nico Pisano in Savona produced 40,000 *maiolica* tiles for the palace of Pope

3.23 The Salón de Baile of the Real Alcázar in Seville with tiled wainscots produced by Cristóbal de Augusta in 1577–9. Reproduced by permission of the Real Alcázar. Courtesy of Arenas Fotografia Artistica, Seville.

Sixtus IV in Genoa. The continuing influence of Spain was felt in the sixteenth century with the local production of tiles of the *arista* type, the use of tiles to cover walls, and the production of painted pictorial panels. The earliest dated example, from 1529, is a panel depicting the Madonna and Child made for the Carretto Palace at Finalmarina, probably by a workshop in Albisola. Trading links between Genoa and Sicily appear to have led to the introduction of the practice there. A panel depicting San Calogero in the grotto of Monte Cronio near Sciacca bears the date 1545. The production of *maiolica* floor tiles was nevertheless well established in Sicily by this time, pavements having been laid in buildings such as the church of San Giorgio at Caltigirone in the later fifteenth century and at the abbey of Monreale around 1520.

In Portugal, the production of painted tin-glazed tiles appears to have begun under the influence of Flemish craftsmen sometime around 1560. Extensive polychrome tilework with finely painted religious and mythological panels set amid ornamental tiles became a feature of the houses of the nobility, such as the Quinta da Bacalhoa in Azeitão (fig. 3.1). Churches too came in for elaborate tiling schemes. For the Igreja São Roque, Francesco de Matos produced panels depicting The Miracle of St Roch set amid a framework of strapwork ornament, these dated 1584. Meanwhile, an ambitious tiled retable wall was produced for the chapel of Nossa Senhora da Vida in the church of Santo André. Now in the Museu Nacional do Azulejo in Lisbon, this scheme incorporates a panel depicting The Adoration of the Shepherds flanked by figures of the evangelists John and

Luke, all set within a *trompe l'oeil* architectural framework. Both this and the mythological panels from the Quinta da Bacalhoa may have been the work of Marçal de Matos, an elder member of the same family.

From the late sixteenth century, plain tiles of different sizes and colours set in chequered patterns made a popular decoration for the walls of Portuguese churches. More common from the early seventeenth century were expansive coverings of painted ornamental tiles, the designs of which often came from textiles. Tiled altar-frontals also borrowed decoration from textiles, including in the middle of the century those brought by the sea-faring Portuguese from India. By the 1670s, however, Portugal's tile-makers were to face major competition from the expanding industries of the Netherlands.

Tile-Stoves

Closed wood-burning stoves have provided a way of heating buildings in central Europe since the thirteenth century. Conical ceramic tiles were inserted into the stone and mortar walls of the stoves in order to increase the radiation of heat. By the fifteenth century, however, these early stoves were replaced by others with walls built entirely from interconnecting ceramic tiles. Initially, niche-type tiles were used, but by the sixteenth century most stoves were constructed from rectangular panel-type tiles. These had deep flanges at the rear to help retain heat, while the front surfaces had relief-moulded decoration enhanced with coloured lead glazes, or else had painted tin-glazed decoration. This latter type became particularly popular in Switzerland and Austria, where the *maiolica* technique was introduced during the sixteenth century.

The typical late medieval tile-stove took the form of a large rectangular fire-box, supported on masonry or legs and topped by a tower to provide a greater surface for the radiation of heat. Though essentially free-standing, the stove would be positioned against a wall in which openings had been cut to connect to a stoke-hole and flue at its rear. This allowed the stove to be stoked directly from an adjacent room, and for fumes to be extracted. The cleanliness of the room in which the stove itself was situated was thus ensured. Only in

3.24 A tile-stove made at Ravensburg in Germany around 1450. The niche-type tiles are made from thrown cylinders cut in two. Height 236cm. V&A. 548-1872.

the eighteenth century did stoves stoked from an opening in the front become standard.

The use of tile-stoves became widespread in the colder climates of central and northern Europe, from Germany, Austria and Switzerland eastwards to Hungary and Poland, and throughout the Baltic regions and Scandinavia. In the fifteenth and sixteenth centuries, stove tiles were also exported from Germany for use in the Netherlands and England, and local manufacture was practised in these countries for a time. Initially, tile-stoves were to be found only in castles, palaces and ecclesiastical buildings, but increasingly they also came to be used in the houses of wealthy citizens. This more widespread use became established in Germany as early as the fourteenth century. In England, where tile-stoves were in any case far less common, they appear to have been confined to royal or ecclesiastical sites until the mid-sixteenth century. Ceramic stoves continue to be used in some parts of Europe.

3.25 A tile-stove made by Hans Kraut of Villengen in Germany, dated 1577, and probably from the Convent of St Wolfgang at Engen. It is composed of panel-type tiles of the typical German relief-decorated type, and others painted on a tin glaze. A variety of religious and allegorical subjects are depicted. Height. 239cm. V&A. 498-1868.

Right: 3.26 The dining-parlour of Greifenzee Castle near Zürich, as depicted in 1643. The Provincial Governor, Hans Bodmer, is seated alongside his wife and children. The room is heated by a large tin-glazed earthenware stove.

Below left: 3.27 A stove tile bearing the mark of its painter, Bartholomaus Dill, and the date 1546. Made in Nuremburg, it is one of a series depicting the story of Jason that is believed to have come from a stove in the house of the Langenmantel family at Tramin near Bolzano. Height. 37.5cm. V&A. C.402-1927.

Below right: 3.28 A stove tile decorated with the Tudor Arms, made at a pottery on the Surrey-Hampshire borders. The inscription 'ER' most probably refers to King Edward VI, dating the tile to around 1550, although it may be from the reign of Elizabeth I. Height. 34.6cm. V&A. C.382-1940.

DELFTWARE AND ITS INFLUENCE

The introduction of tin-glazed earthenware production to the northern provinces of the Netherlands during the sixteenth century might have seemed like just another step in a sequence of migrations of potters. But the scale of the industry that developed was unprecedented, and the pattern of use of tiles was revolutionised. The Golden Age of the Netherlands was indeed a golden age for tiles. The changes that came about in terms of their availability and affordability were enormous. Whereas the *maiolica* floors of sixteenth-century Antwerp had been within the reach of only the wealthiest of clients, painted tiles could be afforded by many of the burghers of the seventeenth-century Dutch cities. Tiles became a ubiquitous and indeed necessary element among the fixtures and fittings of the typical Dutch home.

The startling democratisation of tilework that occurred in the Netherlands during the seventeenth century was the result of several factors. Since the last decades of the previous century, and in spite of the ongoing war with Spain, the thriving mercantile economy had brought a new-found prosperity to the northern provinces. This wealth benefited a broad section of the population and resulted in the formation of a large and prosperous middle class with considerable income at their disposal. Though frequently portrayed as frugal and puritanical, the Dutch burghers were nevertheless happy to spend money on decorating their houses. However, the orderliness and cleanliness of the home was of enormous significance, holding what has been described by the historian Simon Schama as a 'neutralising power over dangerous affluence'. Tiles, being both practical and decorative, came into their own. And, unsurprisingly, the uses to which they were put changed radically.

The most marked change in the use of tiles was the switch from floors to walls. Though tin-glazed tiles had

until then been used primarily on floors, their surface was not hardwearing. Where a householder could afford to improve on the most basic beaten earth floor, they would do so by laying wooden boards or plain red earthenware tiles. Marble or stone, often set in a chequerboard pattern of black and white, was increasingly an option for the more wealthy. Painted tiles, however, provided an ideal surface for decorating areas of wall prone to dirt and damp, this latter problem being particularly acute in the low-lying Netherlands, and especially in the canal-side houses of the Dutch cities. From around 1580, tiles were deployed around fireplaces, on wainscots, along corridors, and most particularly around skirtings (figs 4.3 and 4.8).

Interestingly, this change of use was not accompanied by any immediate changes in the tiles themselves. The wall tile, then, was not a new product, but one that had found a new pattern of use. Nevertheless, a slight reduction in the thickness of tiles can be observed from this point, and gradually new types of decoration more appropriate to the new use appeared. Before the switch to walls occurred, the *maiolica* potters had actually increased their share of the market for floor tiles, competing with the production of lead-glazed inlaid tiles that had persisted since the Middle Ages. As a result, a number of these established tile-makers switched to the production of *maiolica* tiles, while preserving their existing decorative repertoire. Because the

Right: 4.1 The Bath Room at the Water Tower of Carshalton House in Surrey, built in 1719–20 and lined with Dutch tiles (see p 101).

Above: 4.2 A finely painted tile from the De Bloempot factory in Rotterdam, from around 1725–1800. A figure performs upon a stage formed from an elaborate portrait medallion (see p86). 12.8cm sq. V&A. C.128M-1981.

Left: 4.3 'A Woman Peeling Apples', painted by Pieter de Hooch around 1663. Tin-glazed tiles painted with figures adorn the large fireplace and skirting. The Wallace Collection, London.

Right: 4.4 Floor or wall tiles of around 1580–1600, painted in a design derived from inlaid floor tiles. Each 13.7cm sq. V&A. C.477-1923.

inlaid designs were carried out in white clay against a dark background, when replicating them in the *maiolica* technique they had to be painted in reserve, that is, the background rather than the motifs themselves were painted (fig. 4.4). From around 1580 when the tiles began to be used on walls, these essentially Gothic designs were combined with the figurative and more naturalistic motifs derived from Italian and Flemish *maiolica*. Animals, fruit or flowers were set within roundels, quatrefoils or lozenges surrounded by stylised decoration in reserve on a blue ground (fig. 4.5). Though such tiles persisted until around 1640, they were joined early in the seventeenth century by other ornamental polychrome tiles, richly decorated with fruit and flowers, but lacking the decoration in reserve (fig. 4.6). Instead, positively painted corner motifs such as fleur-de-lys began to appear. Initially, the decoration of the tiles still covered the majority of their surfaces. However, over time, both the central and corner motifs became

diminished in size, resulting eventually in the quintessential Dutch tile with a dominant figurative motif in the centre surrounded by an area of undecorated white glaze with small motifs in the corners.

Another feature of the quintessential Dutch tile was its monochrome blue decoration. This new fashion arose under the influence of Chinese porcelain, which had been much in demand in Holland following the capture of two Portuguese cargo ships on their return from the East in 1602 and 1604, and had subsequently been imported by the Verenigde Oost Indische Compagnie (or Dutch East India Company). The fanatical popularity which developed for blue and white ceramics led to the virtual abandonment of polychrome decoration on tiles from around 1625, at least for the urban Dutch market. Chinese-style decorative elements were also copied from the imported wares (fig. 4.7), but, by-and-large, the subjects depicted came from closer to home. Soldiers and cavalrymen, and scenes from

4.5 Four tiles decorated with
birds and animals in lozenges,
from around 1620–40. The
overall effect of the design when
laid is that of a diagonally
disposed chequerboard. Each
13.3cm sq. V&A. C.530-1923.

4.7 Tiles from around 1620–40, decorated with designs copied from Chinese late-Ming porcelain. Each 13.3cm sq. V&A. C.516-1923.

domestic life became hugely popular motifs, as did children's games (figs 4.8, 4.9 and 4.46). This latter group in particular reflected a typically Dutch scrutiny of human nature and folly, and its attendant morality, and were far from being sentimental depictions of childhood. Many of the designs used to decorate tiles were borrowed from printed sources, such as the moralising emblem books produced for the popular market. Flowers, another hugely popular subject, were similarly derived from the popular collections of floral prints known as *florilegia* (figs 4.10 and 4.11). To reproduce the same painted design on a number of tiles, pricked paper patterns were used. The pattern (or *spons*) would be placed over the tile and dusted with charcoal, thus leaving an outline to act as a guide when painting the design. Tiles with figurative decoration seem to have been the most expensive. A set of tiles decorated with foot soldiers and cavalrymen bought in 1634–5 by Sir William Brereton cost nine guilders the hundred, while others decorated with flowers or birds cost only four guilders for the same amount. Plain white tiles would have been cheaper still.

If the importation of Chinese porcelain influenced the decoration of tiles, it also had a profound effect both upon manufacturing technologies and the organisation of the industry. Until the 1620s, production of tiles in the Netherlands had continued in the manner of the sixteenth-century *maiolica* potteries of Antwerp, with a mixed output of tiles and tableware. Haarlem was the first major production centre in the northern provinces. The industry also flourished in Amsterdam from the 1580s. These centres were soon joined by Rotterdam and Delft, and by 1620 the four towns and cities held a roughly equal share of

the market. However, the industry faced a new challenge when imports of Chinese porcelain reached a large scale during the 1620s, the Dutch East India Company supplying a market both in the Netherlands and elsewhere in Europe. The fine quality wares now available were too much for some *maiolica* manufacturers to compete with, and the industry went through a period of decline. The mixed *maiolica* and tile workshops of Haarlem and Amsterdam largely disappeared. However, two of Amsterdam's workshops began specialising in tiles, as did most of the workshops of Rotterdam. In doing so, they avoided the same competition, as the Chinese did not produce tiles.

Most of Delft's workshops took a similar approach, reducing or eliminating tableware manufacture. However, other Delft workshops instead concentrated their efforts on the production of a finer grade of tin-glazed earthenware. The most significant technical development made was in clay preparation. Two clays were used in the production of the wares: a red-firing clay and a chalkier clay or marl. These had to be sufficiently mixed to produce reliable results during firing. However, this was not always achieved by the method of kneading the clays which had previously been used. Instead, a new technique was developed, in which the clays were mixed together in water and then allowed to settle out (fig. 4.44). This method, termed 'washing the clay', produced much better results, and allowed far thinner clay bodies to be produced. Though initially used in the production of tableware, the technique was utilised for tile production from around 1650. The impact was dramatic. Much thinner tiles could be made, the average tile being reduced from around 15mm to 8mm during the course of the century. This made more efficient

4.8 *Kolf Players* painted by Pieter de Hooch in Delft around 1658–60. Behind the door a dado is formed from tiles painted with children playing games. 'Kolf', an early form of golf, was itself often portrayed on such tiles. National Trust Photographic Library. Photographer: Derrick E. Witty.

Below: 4.9 A Dutch tile painted with children playing, of around 1650–1750. The same design, one of an enormous range depicting children's games, can be seen among the tiles shown in De Hooch's *Kolf Players*. 12.7cm sq. V&A. C.6M-1968.

use of raw materials, cut transportation costs, and most significantly, increased the number of tiles that could be fired in the kiln at one time, thus reducing expenditure on fuel and allowing increased production. It was a better product, and one that resulted in savings for both producer and consumer. By the 1660s, simply decorated tiles were available at around twenty-five guilders per thousand. This allowed a tradesman to buy enough tiles to decorate the kitchen-parlour of his home for perhaps three weeks' wages.

Around the middle of the century, however, the market for tiles began to change. Up until then, the demand for tiles had primarily come from the burghers of the Dutch cities, who had been the first to benefit from the country's prosperity. The increasing wealth of this group led to the

Left: 4.10 Tiles depicting tulips and fritillaries, from around 1625–50. The treatment is considerably more naturalistic than earlier types. Each 13.0 cm sq. V&A. C.534-1923.

Right: 4.11 Fritillaries, as illustrated in Crispijn van de Passe's *Hortus Floridus*, published in 1614–16. The design has been copied for use on some of the tiles shown in fig. 4.10. V&A (National Art Library).

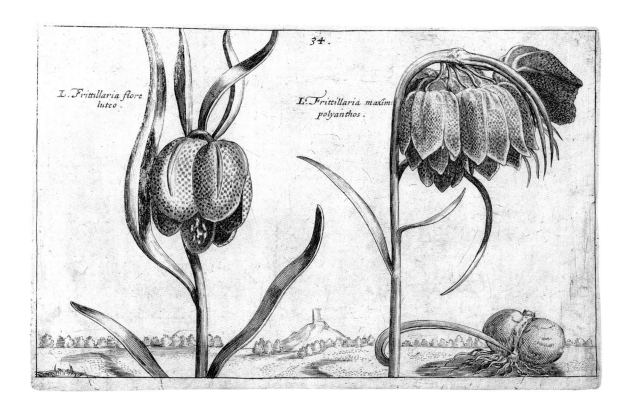

building of larger houses, with cellars and separate kitchens for which tiles with little or no decoration seemed appropriate. The preference in the cities for minimal decoration, however, seems to have been also a question of taste. Increasingly, smaller motifs found favour, and plain white tiling appears to have become popular even in less utilitarian locations, as can be seen in Pieter de Hooch's later paintings of wealthy Amsterdam households. Fireplaces set with plain white Dutch tiles were similarly installed in some of the most opulent rooms of Ham House in London in the 1670s. Meanwhile, a new market for tiles had emerged in the increasingly prosperous rural regions. This new demand encouraged a geographical shift in tile production. Rotterdam remained an important centre but it was joined by the Friesian towns of Harlingen, Makkum and Bolsward, with production also taking place in Amsterdam, Gouda and Utrecht. The richly decorated polychrome tiles, now out of fashion in the cities, found popularity in the rural market. However, this new market also developed its own range of motifs. Not surprisingly, ships and sea creatures were popular subjects in the coastal towns of Friesland (fig. 4.12). And tiles decorated with biblical scenes, which became hugely popular from the end

of the seventeenth century, catered primarily to rural customers. Such tiles provided the typical decoration of the huge tiled fireplaces, known as *smuigers*, found in the rural areas of Noord Holland, north of Amsterdam (fig. 4.13).

The export market also became increasingly important from the mid-seventeenth century. This flourished wherever there was existing coastal trade. Dutch tiles therefore reached northern Germany and Denmark, initially as a return cargo in the trade for cattle, but increasingly as an adjunct to the whaling industry. Similarly, tiles were exported in quantity to northern France, Flanders, Spain and, perhaps most notably, to Portugal. Many of the tiles exported followed the tastes of the rural Dutch markets. However, grand tile pictures also became an important product, particularly for export to Spain and Portugal. Though most Dutch tiles were each decorated with a design complete in itself, tile pictures had been produced in the northern Netherlands as house or shop signs from the end of the sixteenth century (fig. 4.14). From the seventeenth century, tile pictures were also made to decorate the backs of fireplaces, sometimes taking the form of a pair of vertical panels flanking the fire. Ambitious tile panels with allegorical subjects were

Top left: 4.12 Tiles depicting frigates and armed trading ships, probably made in Harlingen around 1650–1700. Some of the designs are copied from prints by Reinier Nooms. Each 13.0cm sq. V&A. C.517 & 569-1923.

Bottom left: 4.13 Tiles painted in purple with biblical subjects. Such tiles were used to cover large wall surfaces and the fronts of the built-in fireplaces known as *smuigers*, which extended from floor to ceiling. Each 13.0cm sq. V&A. C.591-1923.

Above: 4.14 A tiled sign from the façade of the house of a seed dealer in Gorinchem. The panel, which dates from around 1600–25, bears the arms of the city and of the Van Arkel family, along with the legend 'In de 3 Blompotten' (In the 3 Flowerpots). V&A. C.475-1923.

Left: 4.15 A panel painted with allegorical figures of Love, Fidelity, Unity and Steadfastness, bearing the date 1640. Based on a design by Joachim Wtewael for stained glass at St Janskerk in Gouda, the panel was discovered in the nineteenth century in a house occupied by descendants of the Verswaen family who ran the De Swaen workshop. Width approx. 222cm. V&A. C.471-1923.

Right: 4.16 The Convento Madre de Deus in Lisbon, with tile panels produced by the workshop of Jan Van Oort in 1698. Courtesy of Hirmer Verlag, Munich.

produced by the Gouda workshop of De Swaen as early as 1640 (fig. 4.15). However, the grandest pictorial panels were produced for prestigious commissions abroad. Jan Van Oort, who settled in Amsterdam in 1669, produced elaborate painted tiling schemes for churches and palaces in and around Lisbon. The earliest known example is that of the Sala do Panais of the Palácio Fronteira at Benfica, produced between 1670 and 1678. The importation of Dutch tiles in fact reached such levels that in 1687 an embargo was placed upon them in order to protect the local industry. However, exports resumed in 1698, at which time Van Oort fulfilled major commissions for the church of Nossa Senhora da Conceição dos Cardais and the Convento da Madre de Deus, the cloisters of which now house Portugal's Museu Nacional do Azulejo (fig. 4.16).

The leading role in the export trade then passed to Willem van der Kloet's Amsterdam factory De Twee Romeinen (The Two Romans). From the late seventeenth

century, grand panels were also made in a factory on Rotterdam's Delftschevaart. These were painted by Cornelis Boumeester, a specialist in land and seascapes (fig. 4.17). Among Boumeester's works are a series of townscapes incorporated into the extensive tiling of the summer dining room of the Château de Rambouillet near Paris, carried out for Louis XIV's legitimised son Louis-Alexandre, the Compte de Toulouse, around 1715–30. Another Rotterdam factory, that run by the Aelmis family and known as De Bloempot, became a prolific producer of finely painted picture panels during the eighteenth century. Fine panels were also produced in Delft alongside luxury wares. Of particular note are the polychrome flower-vase panels found together with Boumeester's townscapes at Rambouillet, as well as in the kitchen of the Amalienburg pavilion of Schloss Nymphenburg near Munich, built between 1734–9 (fig. 4.18).

The increasingly luxurious wares of Delft had meanwhile attracted a prestigious client in the form of Mary, the English princess who married William of Orange in 1677. Mary had enormous enthusiasm for Delftware, and amassed large collections in her Dutch palaces. A 'cellar kitchen' built for her around 1686 at the Paleis Het Loo at Apeldoorn had walls entirely covered with tiles and seems to have been used by Mary for the display of flowers in an array of Delft vases (fig. 4.19). On William and Mary's accession to the English throne in 1689, Mary took up residence in the Water Gallery, a Tudor building at Hampton Court that had been remodelled in contemporary style by Sir Christopher Wren. Celia Fiennes, who visited soon after 1694, said that the Gallery 'opened into a balcony on to the water and was decked with china and fine pictures'. According to Daniel Defoe, there was also a 'dairy, with all its conveniences, in which the Queen took

great delight'. At the Water Gallery, Mary once again indulged her passion for Delftware, which was presumably in part displayed in the 'Delft-Ware Closett' named in the building accounts. The wares were supplied by Adrianus Kocks of the 'Greek A' factory, and included a number of large tiles and other items painted to the designs of Daniel Marot, a Huguenot artist fully conversant with the latest French architecture and design as sponsored by Louis XIV at Versailles (fig. 4.20). Dutch tiles had in fact already found favour at Versailles, where they had been incorporated into both the interiors and exteriors of the *Trianon de Porcelaine*, a Chinese-style pavilion built in 1670. However, the tiles had been little able to withstand the northern climate and the building was demolished in 1687. The following year, Dutch tiles were used at another of Louis XIV's residences, the Château de Marly at Marly-le-Roi. Here they lined the walls of a bath pavilion.

The combined dominance of French interior design and the growing reputation of Dutch tiles also resulted in the construction of princely tiled rooms elsewhere in Europe. In Germany, the pavilions of Pagodenburg and Badenburg at Schloss Nymphenburg near Munich were constructed for the Elector Maximilian Emanuel between 1716 and 1721. And at Brühl near Cologne, a spectacular hunting lodge, Falkenlust, was built for the Elector Clemens August in 1729–37 (fig. 4.21). Designed by the French architect François Cuvilliés, it incorporated specially commissioned tiles with falconry scenes made at Rotterdam's De Bloempot factory. These were probably to Cuvilliés' own designs. Later, a series of extensively tiled rooms was added to the castle at Brühl. Dutch tiles were also used to decorate Tsar Peter the Great's summer palace at St Petersburg in Russia, while in Poland, extensive tilework was a feature of the palaces of Nieborów and Wilanów.

Left: 4.17 A panel of tiles painted with a hunting scene, made in Rotterdam and signed 'C. BOVMEESTER'. Width approx. 222cm. V&A. C.470-1923.

Right: 4.18 A polychrome tile panel painted with a vase of flowers, made in Delft. Closely related panels were used at Rambouillet and Schloss Nymphenburg. Width approx. 78cm. V&A. C.468-1923.

Above: 4.19 Mary's 'cellar kitchen' at the Paleis Het Loo. The preserving of fruit, then a fashionable occupation for aristocratic ladies, might have been carried out in the kitchen. However, Mary seems to have primarily used the room for the display of flowers. Paleis Het Loo, Apeldoorn, the Netherlands.

Below: 4.20 A large tile from Queen Mary's apartments at Hampton Court. Panels formed from four tiles were probably used to flank a doorway or fireplace, perhaps in the dairy or a closet of the Water Gallery. 61.6cm sq. V&A. C.13-1956.

Right: 4.21 The staircase of the hunting lodge, Falkenlust, lined with tiles painted with falconry subjects. Rheinischen Amt für Denkmalpflege. Photographer: Silvia-Margrit Wolf.

Following pages: 4.22 Equestrian portraits of the Mascarenhas family at the Palácio dos Marqueses de Fronteira near Lisbon. Courtesy of Hirmer Verlag, Munich.

French influence again exerted itself from the late seventeenth century on the decoration of the tiles themselves. This was often observable in the border designs used, but also resulted in the reintroduction of tiles with continuous ornament across their surfaces rather than the usual central motifs. Many of the tiles showing French influence were extremely finely painted (fig. 4.2). Produced as luxury items, such tiles were often exported, though they also found favour in the affluent districts along the Zaan river north of Amsterdam. The pioneering De Bloempot factory seems to have led the way in the introduction of these new designs.

The boom experienced by the Dutch tile industry in the late seventeenth and early eighteenth century came to an end around 1730, and at this time some of the specialist tile factories of Amsterdam and Rotterdam again began production of pottery. Throughout the eighteenth and into the nineteenth century the market for decorated tiles in the Netherlands was predominantly in rural areas. The designs used remained broadly the same throughout this period. Tile pictures, however, became increasingly common, and were incorporated into tiled fireplaces and walls of otherwise plain or simply decorated tiles.

In Portugal, the taste for elaborately painted pictorial panels, later to be sated by Dutch imports, began to grow from the mid-seventeenth century following the War of Restoration in which independence from Spain was reasserted. Opulent new residences, richly decorated with tiles, began to be constructed for the Portuguese nobility. Of these, perhaps the most splendid is the Palácio dos Marqueses de Fronteira in Lisbon, built during 1667–72 (fig. 4.22). Both the interior and exterior of the palace are extensively tiled, as are the numerous architectural features of its gardens. Stone benches are lined with satirical panels depicting monkeys performing human tasks. These are painted in polychrome, though most of the panels from the palace show the new fashion for monochrome blue painting as practised in the Netherlands. A series of arches below a balustraded terrace carry massive equestrian portraits of the Mascarenhas family, owners of the palace. Meanwhile, within the palace are an extraordinary series of panels illustrating the topography and action of battles of the War of Restoration, as well as a group of finely painted mythological scenes carried out in Amsterdam by the workshop of Jan Van Oort around 1670–8.

The increasingly large-scale importation of Dutch tiles created problems for the local industry, whose products, though rich in character, lacked both the technical precision and painterly perfection of the imported tiles.

However, the embargo placed on Dutch tiles in the late seventeenth century allowed the Portuguese workshops breathing space to develop a more competitive product. In addition, the increasing involvement of trained painters in the production of tile panels led to an exceptional period of manufacture in the early to mid-eighteenth century. Leading towards this period of baroque exuberance was the Spaniard Gabrielle del Barco, a painter who settled in Lisbon in 1669 and in time turned exclusively to tile painting. Following at the start of the eighteenth century were Manuel dos Santos, António Pereira and, most notably, António de Oliveira Bernardes, whose workshop dominated production and through which passed a number of other notable tile painters, including Teotónio dos Santos, Nicolau de Freitas and António's son Policarpo. Other great tile painters included Valentim de Almeida, Bartolomeu Antunes and an unknown master who signed his work 'PMP'. The practice of signing work in fact became common during this time, suggesting that the painters perceived a greater status for themselves. However, while their skill is self-evident, it remained standard practice to use engravings as sources rather than produce original designs.

Throughout the period, numerous monumental schemes were executed for the convents, churches and palaces of Portugal and Brazil. Invariably painted in blue, these

4.23 A panel from the Music Room of the Quinta Formosa in Lisbon, around 1720–30. Height 140cm. V&A. C.48-1973.

would cover huge areas of church walls as well as their barrel-vaulted ceilings, while in palaces and grand houses tilework formed a continuous dado around rooms, along corridors and up staircases. Everywhere figurative scenes were set within a framework of *trompe l'oeil* pilasters, caryatids and other architectural ornament (fig. 4.23). New levels of theatricality and playfulness were added by *figuras de convite*, humorously placed to greet and guide guests (frontispiece). These were a speciality of the master PMP, who also helped introduce *fête galante* scenes into the repertoire of the tile painters.

From around 1750, rococo ornament was also introduced, this coinciding with the end of the exclusive use of monochrome blue. Borders of shell-like and foliate rococo motifs, painted in purple, yellow and green, would typically frame figurative scenes in blue. The finest rococo panels were installed at the Palácio de Queluz, particularly along the ornamental canal built in its gardens, and also throughout the gardens of the Quinta dos Azulejos in Lisbon (figs 4.24 and 4.25). The earthquake which devastated Lisbon on 1 November 1755, however, led to a demand for a cheaper product, and tiles decorated with simple patterns began to be made. Nevertheless, rococo panels, and later those with neo-classical ornament, continued to be produced. An important manufacturer in this period was the Real Fábrica do Rato, founded in 1767

4.24 and 4.25 Tile panels depicting 'Olympian Gods' and 'Apollo and Marsyas' from the gardens of the Quinta dos Azulejos, where they flanked a fountain. The panels date from around 1740. The scenes derive from etchings by Michel Dorigny after works by Simon Vouet for the Hôtel Séguier. Height. 272cm. V&A. C.54 & 55-1973.

4.26 The façade of the Hospital de la Santa Caridad in Seville with tile panels dating from around 1660–70.

by the Marquês de Pombal, chief minister to King Joseph I (r.1750–77) and principal planner behind Lisbon's urban reconstruction. In the early nineteenth century, however, production of tiles in Portugal stagnated, a result of the economic decline which followed in the wake of the French invasion and the subsequent departure of the Portuguese royal family to Brazil.

Like Lisbon, Seville was the destination for a number of large Dutch pictorial panels in the later seventeenth century. However, the potters of Triana seem to have been better equipped to compete with the imports than their Portuguese counterparts, and splendid Sevillian tile panels were produced in this period. Of particular note are the panels set on the façade of Seville's Hospital de la Santa Caridad, dating from around 1660–70 (fig. 4.26). Showing Dutch influence in their monochrome blue decoration, the

panels are close in style to the school of Murillo and suggest the involvement of trained painters in their manufacture. Pictorial panels of this type, adorning façades as well as being set into wainscots and typically, though not exclusively, decorated with religious subjects, were at this time gaining in popularity over the traditional wainscots with continuous ornamental decoration across their surface for the decoration of churches and important buildings. Tilework was, however, increasingly available to a wider market. This led to the proliferation of small devotional panels, frequently set on the façades of buildings. However, the most popular type produced by the potters of Triana during the eighteenth century were tiles decorated with a single motif, typically set within a roundel with a blue border (fig. 4.27). Such tiles clearly owed a great deal to Flemish and Dutch prototypes, yet with these tiles the potters of Seville appear to have dominated the local market, leaving no room for the imports of mass-produced Dutch tiles which reached other cities of southern Spain, such as Cadiz.

Though probably suffering as a result of the difficult economic climate of mid-seventeenth-century Spain, other production centres such as Toledo and Talavera continued tile production throughout the seventeenth century. One of Talavera's more notable potters, Ignacio Mansill del Pino, even received a commission for 10,000 tiles for the Royal Palace in Madrid. However, Spanish tile production began to be dominated first by Catalonia, and then by Valencia. Production in Catalonia, which was based primarily around Barcelona, was split between the large-scale manufacture of standard tiles with ornamental patterns or increasingly with individual motifs, and the manufacture of pictorial panels, the grandest of which would be made for special commissions. A particular type of single motif tile was developed in the region, the so-

4.27 A tile made at Triana, the principal pottery manufacturing district in Seville, around 1750–1800. 13.8cm sq. V&A. C.1185-1919.

Top: 4.28 Catalan *rajoles de oficis*,
from the late eighteenth or early
nineteenth century. Each approx.
13.2cm sq. V&A. C.756, 757, 759,
761, 764 & 765-1920.

Above: 4.29 Valencian tiles of
around 1750–1800, painted with
hunting or rural scenes. Height
approx. 12.3cm.
V&A. 431 & 432-1905.

4.30 A tiled kitchen from Valencia. The vividly painted *trompe l'oeil* tilework creates its own interior bustling with activity. Courtesy of Museo Nacional de Artes Decorativas, Madrid.

called *rajoles de oficis*, which as the name suggests are decorated with figures representing trades, but also with saints, mythological figures, animals and other figures and emblems (fig. 4.28). With the exception of some early examples decorated in blue, these *rajoles de oficis* had polychrome decoration with a distinctive yellow band around the edge. Such tiles were enormously popular throughout the eighteenth and into the nineteenth century.

Of those tile pictures produced, the most splendid are perhaps the two lunette-shaped panels made for a house in Alella owned by the Marquis of Castellvell and now in the Museu de Ceràmica in Barcelona. The first of these lively and colourful panels depicts a bullfight, while the other shows a 'chocolate party' where elegant ladies and gentlemen take supper, drink chocolate, dance and promenade. Such genteel subject matter is typical of the French influence that permeated Spain following the entrance of the Bourbon dynasty in 1714.

In Valencia, a specialised tile industry developed within

the city itself during the seventeenth century, while the production of earthenwares continued at nearby Manises. By 1750, Valencia was Spain's major production centre. Various notable workshops were in operation at this time, including those of Vicente Navarro in the Calle de la Corona, and of the Ferrán family in the Calle de las Barcas. Like the Catalonian *rajoles de oficis*, Valencia developed its own type of genre tile. These tiles, which had no borders and tended to be of rectangular shape, were painted with figures in landscapes so as to form a continuous horizon along a row (fig. 4.29). They were often placed on the risers of stairs, though as was the case elsewhere in Spain, this was just one of an immense variety of uses to which tiles were put. As well as various settings on walls, stairs and balconies, in Valencia painted tiles also remained popular for floors. One exceptional example was laid in the Galería Dorada of the Ducal Palace in Gandía by 1714. A square room divided radially, the floor is composed of a series of trapezoidal tiles of varying sizes, and carries a complex allegorical design symbolising the four Elements. Later in the century, Valencian tiled floors were singled out for special praise from Joseph Townsend, a Rector from Wiltshire who travelled to Spain in 1786–7: 'I was most delighted with the manufacture of painted tiles. In Valencia, their best apartments are floored with these, and are remarkable for neatness, for coolness, and for elegance. They are stronger and much more beautiful than those we formerly received from Holland.' Praise indeed.

Another remarkable phenomenon of Valencian tilework was that of the tiled kitchen decorated with *trompe l'oeil* scenes of culinary activity. These charming interiors are close in spirit to the *figuras de convite* of Portugal, and indeed *trompe l'oeil* tilework for kitchens was also produced there. One of the most splendid examples can be found in the Museo Nacional de Artes Decorativas in Madrid (fig. 4.30). Meticulously painted tiles were also among the luxurious products of the Real Fabrica del Alcora in the Castellon region to the north of Valencia. Founded in 1727 on the initiative of the Conde de Aranda, this entirely new and highly organised factory was a producer of high-quality tin-glazed earthenware in a French style.

Some of the most extravagant of late baroque tilework was to be found in Naples. Here, carpet-like schemes, painted with bold linear ornament incorporating oval cartouches, acanthus scrolls, volutes and floral swags adorned the floors of churches and prestigious apartments. A fine example is the pavement of the luxurious prior's quarters of the Carthusian Certosa di San Martino, made by the workshop of Giuseppe Massa and dated 1741. Around

the same time, the Massa workshop also produced the tilework of the cloister garden of the convent of Santa Chiara (fig. 4.31). Here the hexagonal columns of an elaborate pergola were faced with tiles painted so as to form spiralling garlands, while tiled benches were set with panels painted with landscapes. Another important Neapolitan tile-maker, Leonardo Chiaiese, produced one of the most spectacular of all *maiolica* pavements at the church of San Michele Arcangelo in Anacapri in 1761. The entire floor is given over to a vast pictorial composition depicting The Expulsion of Adam and Eve from Paradise. So monumental is the scale of this work, it can only be fully appreciated from a considerable height. Another extraordinary achievement of Neapolitan ceramics was the *Salottino di Porcellana*, a room lined with porcelain tiles painted in *chinoiserie* style created for the Palazzo Reale in Pórtici between 1757 and 1759. This unusual example of porcelain as a material for tilework was made at the Capodimonte factory. Elsewhere in Italy, at the major production centres such as Faenza and Deruta, tile manufacture continued as a sideline to the production of tableware.

In Germany, France and Scandinavia, the demand for Dutch tiles prompted local manufacture based on Dutch prototypes. Such enterprises frequently involved craftsmen from the Netherlands. In Germany, tiles were being made by the late seventeenth century at the tin-glazed earthenware potteries established in Hanau and Frankfurt am Main. The Delft potter Johann Kaspar Rib, who was active at the Frankfurt factory in 1702–8, later became involved with production at Brunswick, Nuremberg and Zerbst. Tiles were also among the products of factories such as those at Erfurt, Ansbach, Kellinghusen, Berlin and also Potsdam, from where Carl Friedrich Lüdicke supplied tiles to Catherine II of Russia in 1776. However, despite occasional prestigious commissions, tiles remained only a minor element of production. In Denmark, tin-glazed tiles were first made at the Store Kongensgade in Copenhagen, founded in 1723. Meanwhile, tiles were among the products of Sweden's first tin-glazed pottery manufactory, Rörstrand, established in 1726. In France, simple but lively tin-glazed tiles were produced in Lille and elsewhere in the north-east, such as Vron, Douai, Saint-Omer, Desvres and Saint-Armand-les-Aux. The decoration of tiles at all these various centres conformed by-and-large to the models provided by the Dutch imports, though achieving varying degrees of refinement. In Russia, tin-glazed stove tiles decorated in blue in a Dutch style were made from the early eighteenth century, initially at the behest of Tsar Peter I. Of more local character are the tiles painted predominantly in green and brown with figurative and *chinoiserie* scenes made there later in the century.

In England, the production of tin-glazed floor tiles established at Aldgate in the later sixteenth century was continued at a number of other London potteries in the early seventeenth century. Hugh Cressey and Edmund Bradshaw of the Montague Close pottery in Southwark obtained a patent for the manufacture of 'paving tiles of all Sises' in 1613, though Cressey later claimed this to have been infringed by Samuel Sotherne who was alleged to have made 'great quantities of pavinge tyles'. Then, in 1628, exclusive rights to the production of tin-glazed earthenware and tiles for a twenty-one-year period were acquired by Christian Wilhelm of the Pickleherring pottery, also in Southwark. Wilhelm claimed to have been in production for sixteen years, though perhaps did so for the purposes of challenging Cressey's patent.

By the mid-seventeenth century, however, there was clearly a demand in England for wall tiles of the modern Dutch type, particularly for use in fireplaces. There was also a wider demand for Dutch tin-glazed pottery (or 'Delftware' as it became known), the importation of which challenged the local industry to the extent that in 1672 four London potters were successful in obtaining a royal proclamation banning it. The following year, a bill, later rejected, came before Parliament to further protect the interests of the English potters. This met with considerable opposition from the so-called Glass Sellers (the retailers of the wares) who complained that: 'The Potters made dishes and painted wares, but not the sixth part of what the shopkeepers vend. He could have no tiles from them, though he had waited long for them. They could not supply him.' Tiles were, incidentally, sold by the 'foot', meaning four tiles of the standard 5-inch size covering an area of rather less than a square foot.

The first painted tin-glazed wall tiles comparable to contemporary Dutch products that were made in England seem to have been the work of Jan Ariens van Hamme, who arrived from Delft in 1676 with his family and sixteen workmen, and established a pottery at Vauxhall in London (fig. 4.32). Van Hamme made the somewhat extravagant claim that he intended to make 'Tiles . . . and other earthenwares after the way practised in Holland which hath not been practised in this our kingdom.' However, he seems to have experienced initial technical difficulties. A letter from one Dr William Johnson in 1677 stated: 'The

4.31 Extensive tilework in the gardens of the convent of Santa Chiara in Naples, made by the workshop of Giuseppe Massa around 1740. Photo Scala, Florence.

The tiles, from top left to bottom right, are captioned:

The Plot first hatcht at Rome by the Pope and Cardinalls &c.

The Conspirators Signeing ye Resolve for killing the King.

Father Connyers Preaching against ye Oathes of Alejance & Supremacy.

Dr Oates discovereth ye Plot. to ye King and Councell.

Ct bedlow discoverer of the plott.

Capt. bedlow examind by ye secret Comitee of the house of Commons.

Pickerin attempts to kill ye K. in St Iames Park.

Pickerin Executed.

St William waller burning Popish books Images .and Reliques.

4.32 Nine tiles made in London around 1679–80, possibly by the workshop of Jan Ariens van Hamme. The tiles depict the 'Popish Plot', a fictitious Catholic conspiracy to kill Charles II which the Revd Titus Oates claimed to have uncovered in 1678. Each approx. 12cm sq. V&A. 414:823-1885.

day after my coming to the City . . . I went to Lambeth and Vauxhall to enquire about the tiles, but found them in both places unfurnished, they telling me they were yet at a loss both in the mixture of their clay and way of burning them.' Johnson went on to seek out Dutch tiles instead, which were still available despite the reinforcement in 1676 of the earlier ban on imports. Van Hamme died in 1680, and though tile production seems to have continued to increase in London, there was an apparent shortage of skilled labour. In 1718, Thomas Oade described how he had brought a Dutch potter to his father Nathaniel's pottery in Gravel Lane, Southwark, stating that tiles for fireplaces were 'a very beneficial part of the Trade, and not a Man in the Kingdom to be got, that could make them to any purpose'. By 1726, however, an inventory of that pottery recorded the presence of 12,886 tiles, indicating that production was being carried out on a considerable scale.

From around 1720, then, it seems that tiles became a standard product of many of the delftware potteries concentrated along the south bank of the Thames. They were certainly produced at Vauxhall, Lambeth High Street, Glasshouse Street and Norfolk House. They were also a product of the Liverpool factories, being made from the outset at Lord Street, the city's first delftware pottery which opened in 1710. In Bristol, England's third great delftware production centre, tiles were made in at least two factories: Limekiln Lane and Redcliff Back. They were also known to have been produced at the Delftfield pottery in Glasgow, in Wincanton, and possibly in Belfast.

Though not deployed as extensively as in the Netherlands, tin-glazed tiles found a wide variety of uses in England and Scotland. Of these, by far the most common setting was in the sides of fireplaces. William Brereton had used Dutch tiles in this way in 1634–5, also setting them in the hearth, while the diarist Samuel Pepys had fireplaces 'done with Dutch tiles' in 1666. As English tin-glazed tiles became available they would have been used in the same way. A trade card for the china dealer John Gulliford, for example, offers for sale 'White and Painted Tiles for Chimneys' in 1736 (fig. 4.33). Few survive *in situ* in fireplaces but examples can be found at Wordsworth House in Cumbria and Pollok House in Glasgow (fig. 4.34), while printed tin-glazed tiles appear in a fireplace at Croft Castle in Herefordshire (fig. 4.35). Tin-glazed tiles seem occasionally to have been used as skirtings in England, as was common in the Netherlands. In the Bristol area, tiled recesses housing wash-basins were installed in small closets adjacent to elegant dining rooms (fig. 4.36). Tin-glazed tiles were also used to line cold baths (fig. 4.1) and to cover the

4.33 The trade card of John Gulliford of Southwark, bearing the date 1736 (or 1730). 'Painted Tiles for Chimneys' are advertised, and blocks of plain and painted tiles are shown flanking the sign. V&A. E.2358-1987.

walls of genteel dairies (see pp110–11). Meanwhile, Daniel Defoe considered them to be an essential attribute of shop interiors. Writing in 1710, he described the ideal fittings for a pastry cook's shop as having 'all the walks of the shop lin'd with galley-tiles, and the Backshop with galley-tiles in pannels, finely painted in forest-work and figures'. Though this description is somewhat opaque, a number of known painted tile panels can be associated with commercial premises (fig. 4.37).

In the earlier part of the eighteenth century, the decoration of tiles followed Dutch prototypes and bore monochrome decoration in blue or, less commonly, purple. Landscapes were popular, as were biblical scenes, which were copied either from illustrated bibles or directly from Dutch tiles. Other forms of decoration, such as the use of powdered pigment to produce a coloured ground, also probably arrived via the Netherlands. However, by the middle of the century, decoration distinct from Dutch

4.34 The fireplace in the Red Bedroom of Pollok House in Glasgow. Powdered and painted tiles, probably from Glasgow's Delftfield pottery, line the sides of the fireplace above a typical eighteenth-century hob grate. The National Trust for Scotland.

prototypes began to appear, with different production centres developing their own types, this nevertheless being somewhat blurred by the movement of potters between potteries and the copying of styles. Many fine polychrome tiles, including those painted in the so-called *Fazackerly* palette and others bearing genteel scenes, can be associated with Liverpool (fig. 4.38). Meanwhile, the Swede Magnus Lundberg seems to have introduced from Rörstrand the use of *bianco-sopra-bianco* border decoration, with painting in white on a blue-tinged glaze, first bringing the technique to London and then Bristol (fig. 4.39).

The most dramatic developments in the decoration of delftware occurred in Liverpool in the 1750s, when John Sadler and Guy Green developed a process for transferring a printed image onto tiles. This seems to have been done by means of a glue 'bat', a gelatinous and flexible pad of animal glue which was first placed on a woodblock or engraved copper plate charged with oil, and then onto a glazed and fired tile. Once the bat had been carefully removed, the oil left on the surface of the tile could then be dusted with pigment. This was followed by a third firing in

a 'muffle' kiln, at the lower temperature of around 760°C (a process also on occasion used to fire additional colours unable to withstand the second 'glost' firing). Tiles decorated in this way could be produced quickly and cheaply, yet with extremely fine decoration (fig. 4.40). In Sadler and Green's famous affidavit of 1756, they stated that: 'on Tuesday the 27th day of July instant, they these deponents, without the aid or assistance of any other person or persons, did within the space of six hours . . . print upwards of twelve hundred earthenware tiles of different patterns . . . more in number, and better, and neater than one hundred skilful pot painters could have painted in a like space of time'. The economic implications of this were considerable. A certificate by Thomas Shaw and Samuel Gilbody in support of Sadler and Green's claim commented that the tiles 'may be sold at little more than half the price [of painted tiles] . . . [and] that as the Dutch (who import large quantities of tiles into England, Ireland, etc) may by this improvement be considerably undersold, it cannot fail to be of great advantage to the nation, and to the towne of Liverpoole in particular'.

4.35 A fireplace at Croft Castle in Herefordshire, decorated with tiles printed by Sadler and Green in Liverpool around 1765–75. National Trust Photographic Library. Photographer: J. Whitaker.

Left: 4.36 A wash-basin recess
with four niches, reputedly from
a house in Bristol and dating
from around 1725–50. The niches
would likely have held candles.
Each tile 12.5cm sq.
V&A. C.13-1980.

Right: 4.37 A tile panel depicting
St Mary Redcliffe Church in
Bristol, probably made at Richard
Frank's pottery at Redcliff Back,
Bristol, around 1745–50. The
panel was found set in the wall
of a ham and bacon merchant's
shop in the city. Height 52cm.
V&A. 3144-1901.

Sadler and Green began commercial production around 1756–7, rapidly exchanging woodblocks for copper plates on account of their finer quality prints. The product was a success, produced large profits, and reached markets as far afield as America. Various rococo designs were made, as well as other scenes of genteel and rustic life, fables, and later a range of neo-classical designs and theatrical portraits (fig. 4.41). Green continued production after Sadler's retirement in 1770, while production was also carried out in the 1770s by Richard Abbey, a former apprentice.

As well as tin-glazed earthenware tiles, from 1761 Sadler printed creamware for Josiah Wedgwood. This exceptionally fine, new and pale-coloured earthenware was revolutionising tableware production in Staffordshire. By 1767, Wedgwood was considering using the material for tile manufacture, writing to his future partner Bentley that: 'Cream-colour Tyle are much wanted, & the consumption will be great for Dairys, Baths, Summer Houses, Temples &c &c' (see pp110–11). Their production does not, however, appear to have started until around 1776 when Wedgwood described them as 'a fine wholesale Article, as a

bath will take 4 or 500 doz to furnish it, & Mr Green allows us a good profit upon them'. Both plain and printed or over-glaze painted creamware tiles were produced by Wedgwood in the late eighteenth and early nineteenth century, many of the patterns used being derived from tableware border designs. Creamware tiles were also produced by other manufacturers. In 1789, for example, Greens Bingley & Co, operating from the Swinton pottery in Leeds, supplied '700 best Vine Leaf Enameld Tyles' along with 1,730 plain creamware tiles to the home of the Rt Hon. Lionel Damer in Dorset. In connection with the order, the company wrote that 'we . . . do not doubt but the Quality will give Mr Damer entire satisfaction'. Production of creamware tiles seems, however, to have remained on a relatively modest scale. Nevertheless, the massive popularity of creamware for the table sounded the death-knell for the English delftware industry. By default, this also brought an end to the manufacture of tin-glazed tiles in England, which had never been produced in specialist tile factories but alongside other tin-glazed wares. Few delftware potteries survived beyond 1780–5.

Top left: 4.38 A tile depicting a couple out walking, made in Liverpool around 1758–75. 12.6cm sq. V&A. C.536-1922.

Top right: 4.40 A tile depicting a gallant offering a girl a bird's nest, printed in Liverpool by John Sadler, around 1758–61. 12.8cm sq. V&A. C.138-1981.

Above: 4.39 Tiles with chinoiserie designs and *bianco-sopra-bianco* borders, probably made at Richard Frank's pottery at Redcliff Back, Bristol, around 1760–70. Each approx. 12.5cm sq. V&A. C.46B&E-1960.

4.41 A panel of tiles printed in black and over-painted in green, depicting neo-classical subjects including the Four Seasons and Three Graces. Printed in Liverpool, probably by Guy Green, around 1770–80. Each pictorial tile approx. 12.4cm sq. V&A. C.326-1930.

A Delftware Factory

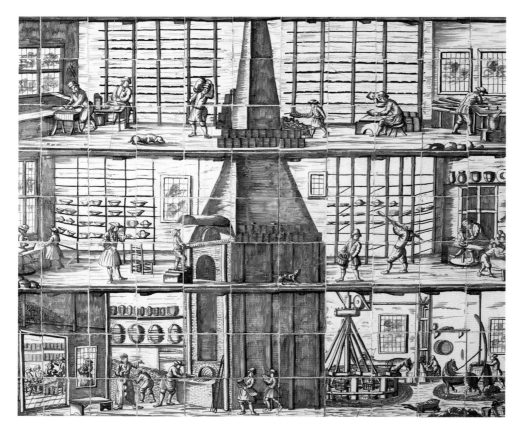

Left: 4.42 A tile panel painted with a cross-section of the Bolsward factory in Friesland, dated 1737. On the ground floor, horses power a pug-mill (for mixing clay) and a glaze grinder, while pottery and tile painters work in a separate room to the left. On the first floor, pottery is being made, while at either end of the top floor, tiles are formed in wooden frames, before being cut square and stacked to dry close to the chimney. The kiln itself dominates the building. On the first floor, a boy watches the progress of the firing through a spy-hole. © Rijksmuseum Amsterdam.

Below: 4.43 The façade of Griffith's Lambeth High Street pottery in London, as shown in a watercolour of around 1850. A panel of painted tin-glazed tiles, no doubt made by the firm, provided decoration over the doorway. Courtesy of London Metropolitan Archives.

The delftware factories of the Netherlands and England brought new levels of industrialisation to ceramic production. Despite a certain amount of specialisation, more often than not tiles were produced alongside other wares. Vast quantities of tiles were produced and wastage rates were high: perhaps only 25 per cent of tiles survived the manufacturing process in perfect condition, though many of the rest were saleable as seconds. Wastage rates for tiles were particularly high as they were placed directly in the kiln rather than loaded into the cylindrical saggars which offered some protection from the intensity of the fire.

Most factories employed a workforce of upwards of twenty-five or thirty men. The whole operation was overseen by a pot-house manager, who might also be the factory owner. He would be assisted by a clerk, who acted both as a deputy and a financial manager. The employees of next most important rank were the pottery painters who, owing to their slower speed of work, outnumbered the potters actually making the tiles and wares by around two to one. Around eight to ten painters would have been required to decorate enough pottery to fill a kiln that was fired once every two to three weeks. The factory would also employ a clay-cellar manager, two or three kiln-men and a variety of other labourers and apprentices.

The kiln itself would have been of the traditional wood-fired up-draught type, larger but otherwise little changed from those used in Italy in the sixteenth century. The loading of the kiln, itself a skilled task, took two days. Tiles were packed at the

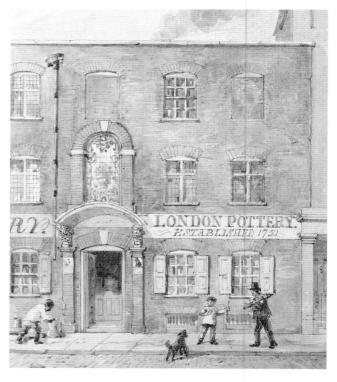

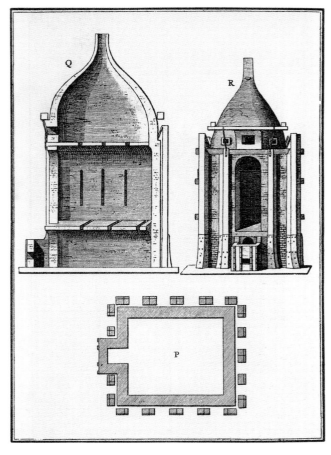

Above left: 4.44 The first stage in clay preparation, 'The washing of the clay', as illustrated by Paape in 1794. The clays were mixed together in water (as shown at A) and then sieved into shallow beds where the clay was allowed to settle out. It was then cut into blocks and stored ready for use. Various tools used in the process are also shown. V&A.

Above right: 4.45 The typical kiln, as illustrated by Paape in 1794. The kiln was loaded through the tall arch, which was bricked up before firing. At the base of the kiln, the firing chamber can be seen. V&A.

Right: 4.46 A tile painted with a cavalryman, made in the Netherlands around 1650–1700.

The tile is a second: the glaze in the top-left corner has run, obscuring the design. The downward flow of the glaze shows that it was fired standing on its edge. 12.7cm sq. V&A. 8-1871

bottom, with those receiving their first 'biscuit' firing beneath those which had already been biscuit-fired, glazed and decorated. The tiles were placed in rows back to back and face to face, and held upright by strips of clay lightly pressed down along the tops of the rows. Firing would take around thirty-six hours, the kiln reaching a temperature of between 980°C and 1,000°C. In Friesland and also in Liverpool, peat was sometimes used to fuel the kiln. The firing was the most important event in the life of the factory. Profits and livelihoods depended upon it. Perhaps reflecting this, on the night of firing the workers in the Liverpool factories were, according to Joseph Mayer, 'always allowed potatoes to roast at the kiln fires, and a certain quantity of ale to drink'. After firing, the kiln required two days to cool before being unloaded.

Dairies

During the eighteenth and nineteenth centuries it was fashionable to construct ornamental dairy buildings on the great estates. The prettification of these dairies belied their practical function: to supply the household with butter, cream, milk and sometimes cheese. That they were typically the most ornamented of estate farm buildings was due to the frequent involvement of the lady of the house. Indeed, the management of the dairy was seen as a highly appropriate female pastime, and came to be associated with romantic notions of goodness and simplicity. The dairy buildings themselves often also served secondary interests of the women, housing collections of china or shells, for example.

Milk would be brought daily to the dairy and poured into shallow pans to allow the cream to settle. This was then skimmed off and churned into butter. Cream would keep fresh for up to five days, according to the season; butter was freshly churned each day. In order to keep the produce fresh, it was essential to maintain a cool and even temperature. Various measures were taken in the design of the dairies in order to achieve this, including sunken floors, insulated cavity walls or thatched roofs, stained glass or verandas to reduce sunlight, as

Top right: 4.47 The dairy at Howsham Hall in Yorkshire was richly decorated with mid-eighteenth-century English tin-glazed earthenware tiles. Country Life Picture Library.

Top left: 4.48 The dairy at Berrington Hall, built around 1783 in neo-classical style. Plain tin-glazed tiles are bordered by others printed with a Greek key pattern by Guy Green in Liverpool. National Trust Photographic Library. Photographer: Nadia MacKenzie.

Bottom left: 4.49 The dairy at Ham House, London, with plain and vine-leaf patterned Wedgwood creamware tiles. Victorian ice-cream making equipment can be seen on the shelf. National Trust Photographic Library. Photographer: Andreas von Einsiedel.

Right: 4.50 Minton tiles and architectural faïence create a rich interior at the Royal Dairy at Frogmore, Windsor, built for Queen Victoria and Prince Albert in 1858–61. The Royal Collection © HM Queen Elizabeth II.

well as running water or fountains. Many of these clearly also had ornamental qualities. Tiles were an ideal material for lining the dairy walls, helping to keep the building cool, being easy to keep clean, and also being suitably decorative. Tin-glazed tiles were employed in the early to mid-eighteenth century, but by the 1780s creamware tiles had taken their place, with Wedgwood seemingly holding something of a monopoly on both tiles and dairy equipment.

Dairies were built in an endless variety of styles, ranging from Gothic to neo-classical, vernacular to Moorish. They nevertheless shared many of the same features. Typically, the dairy would be equipped with a wide marble or slate surface built around the room to hold the milk pans and cream vases. Often a marble-topped table would stand in the centre. In addition to the main interior space, most had a smaller room with a copper for boiling water to sterilise the dairy equipment. Some also had a separate churning room. The fashion for ornamental dairies, well established in Britain by the mid-eighteenth century, was also taken up in France, most famously by Marie Antoinette at the Petit Trianon in Versailles.

INDUSTRIES AND REVIVALS

The history of tilework in the nineteenth and twentieth centuries is one of industrialisation, innovation, stylistic eclecticism and revival. The whole period is characterised by the combination of looking forward, with new technologies, greater efficiency and increased awareness of health and hygiene, and looking back, through the rehabilitation of past styles and techniques and the shaping of a vision of the past to fit the times. For much of the nineteenth century, Britain played a central role in the development of the tile industry. That these innovations largely stemmed from one country might be considered remarkable. That they were, almost without exception, connected with a single manufacturer is extraordinary. Yet, as the pioneering ceramic historian Llewellynn Jewitt wrote in 1878, 'The history of encaustic and other tiles by Minton, Hollins & Co. is the history of the entire modern trade in these useful and beautiful articles.' And the 'entire modern trade' by 1878 was considerable.

The first steps towards the great tile industry of the nineteenth century, though certainly taken with commercial interests in mind, cannot have appeared especially promising. Few could have guessed at the explosion of production and consumption that would follow. The beginnings of the new industry lay in the reinvention of a medieval technique, prompted by a mixture of antiquarian curiosity and the market potential associated with church building and restoration. According to Jewitt, Herbert Minton had turned his attention to inlaid tiles in 1828, but it was Samuel Wright who patented their manufacture in 1830. Yet although Wright put his tiles into production,

and they received praise in J.C. Loudon's *Encyclopaedia of Cottage, Farm and Villa Architecture* in 1833, the venture does not seem to have been a commercial success. By 1836 he had sold his moulds and a share of his patent rights to Minton, who agreed to pay ten per cent royalties on all tiles sold. Wright's remaining stock of tiles must have been included in the deal, as Minton apparently used these in 1837 to fulfil the commission for the hall pavement of Kilmory Castle at Lochgilphead in Argyll.

Considerable experimentation was in fact required by Minton before he perfected the technique, throughout which he displayed his characteristic tenacity and determination, regardless of the costs entailed. When his partner Robert Boyle raised objections, he is reputed (again according to Jewitt) to have said, 'Say no more on the subject, Mr. Boyle. I will make these tiles if they cost me a guinea each!' Minton does not appear to have been in a position to market his inlaid tiles much before 1841, when he supplied several churches and received his first major commission for the pavement of the Temple Church in London. For this, Minton based his

Right: 5.1 The Central Lobby of the Palace of Westminster with inlaid floor tiles designed by Pugin and made by Minton & Co. The Central Lobby was among the first parts of the new building to be completed, and was opened with the House of Lords in 1847 (see p116). By permission of the Palace of Westminster.

Above: 5.2 Tile-making at Worcester, from an illustrated account of a visit to the Chamberlain works published in the *Penny Magazine*, February 1843. The press used to force the clay into the mould as shown. The impressed design was apparently filled by plastering on 'honey-like clay ... using a kind of knife or trowel'. V&A.

Left: 5.3 Tiles from Alton Towers, designed by Pugin and made by Minton & Co. around 1842–4. Pugin reputedly made drawings for tiles during his many journeys on the night train from London to Staffordshire while engaged in works for the Earl of Shrewsbury. Each approx. 14.7cm sq. V&A. C.224 to 227-1993.

Right: 5.4 Tiles from the sanctuary of St George's Roman Catholic Cathedral in Southwark. The damage to the tiles occurred during bombing raids in 1941 which destroyed substantial parts of the building. Designed by Pugin, such tiles had earlier been used at the church of St Giles, Cheadle. Total width approx. 54cm. V&A. C.1 to D-1978.

designs on the tiles of the recently uncovered thirteenth-century pavement in the chapter house of Westminster Abbey (fig. 1.10).

Minton was not, however, the first to successfully manufacture inlaid tiles based on medieval prototypes. A downturn in trade in the mid-1830s had prompted Walter Chamberlain to look for ways to diversify production at his highly accomplished Worcester porcelain manufactory. This, coupled with the potential prestige afforded by association with the county's rich tradition of medieval tilework, persuaded him likewise to buy into Wright's patent. Production may have begun as early as 1836–7, and continued following Chamberlain's buyout of the other great Worcester porcelain maker, Flight, Barr & Barr, in 1840. Though the tiles were usually marked 'Chamberlain & Co.', a catalogue published in 1844 used the style 'F. St John, G. Barr, & Co.', reflecting the fact that George Barr and Fleming St John were by then the principal parties involved with tile production, which since the merger had

transferred to the old Flight, Barr & Barr works. It was also in 1844 that Wright's initial patent was to expire. This he successfully renewed for a further seven years before immediately disposing of it in equal shares to Minton and St John. The tiles made by the Worcester firm were of good quality and closely followed their medieval antecedents, among which were many of the Great Malvern school. Yet with Minton increasingly dominating the market, production appears to have been abandoned and the business sold to Maw & Co. in 1850.

Though based on a medieval technique, the inlaid tiles of the nineteenth century (or *encaustics* as they became known) were made using different processes (see also p.152). Whereas medieval inlaid tiles are thought to have been stamped using carved wooden blocks in order to produce the necessary patterns in counter-relief, in the nineteenth century the tiles were moulded. The usual method was to use a screw-press to force the clay onto a plaster mould set within a metal frame (fig. 5.2). Sometimes

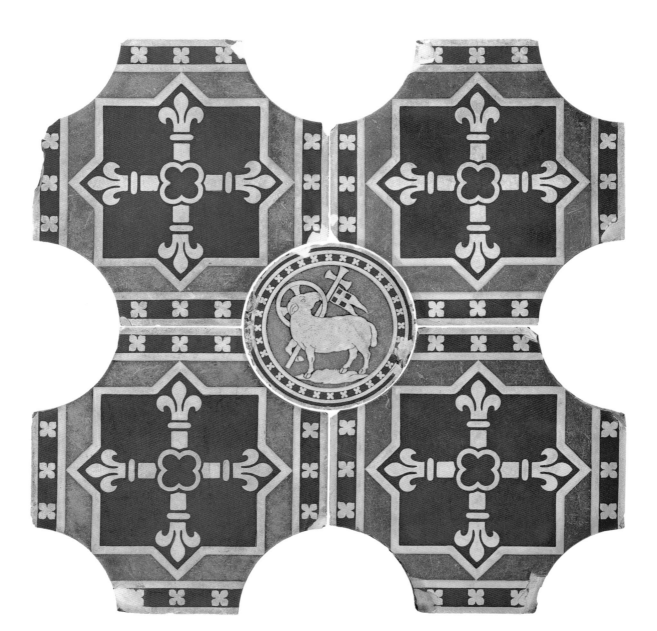

a thin layer of fine buff clay was pushed in ahead of the coarser red body clay, followed by a second layer of fine clay. This provided a fine surface, while the sandwich structure prevented warping. The impressions formed were then filled with clay slip, this being allowed to dry before scraping the surface of the tile level. The design would then appear sharply against the surrounding clay. After a further period of drying, the tiles were fired, and if required, glazed and fired once more. One of the principal difficulties lay in the uneven shrinkage of inlay and body clay during the firing, and this would result in cracks or the loss of the inlay. This was no doubt the major obstacle that Minton and the other manufacturers had to overcome.

In the early 1840s, the demand for paving tiles for churches undergoing restoration was growing, yet at the same time there was increasing concern that appropriate designs be used. The publication in 1841 of the first instalment of John Gough Nichols' *Examples of Decorative Tiles, Sometimes Termed Encaustic*, sought to make available a range of medieval tile designs and to encourage architects to use appropriate tiles for church restorations. Nichols' pioneering work also appears to have established a model for the printed catalogues of the tile manufacturers, the first of which was published by Minton in 1842: *Examples of Old English Tiles* showed designs based on the Westminster Chapter House tiles, as well as others designed by A.W.N. Pugin for the Earl of Shrewsbury for use at Alton (fig. 5.3). All these designs employed a buff inlay on a dark (usually red) ground, thus following medieval example. Under the influence of Pugin, however, this was set to change dramatically. Pugin produced tile designs in connection with a number of prestigious architectural commissions upon which he was working and for which Minton supplied the tiles. Among these was the church of St Giles, Cheadle, constructed around 1846 for the Earl of Shrewsbury (fig. 5.4), but most celebrated of all were the interiors of the new Palace of Westminster (fig. 5.1). Pugin had assisted Charles Barry in the preparation of his winning entry in the competition to design the new building, following the destruction by fire in 1834 of the medieval palace. In 1844, Barry again enlisted Pugin's help, this time to design the interior fittings, among which pavements of Minton tiles featured prominently.

When the House of Lords opened in 1847, it was to great acclaim. The building and its decoration are masterpieces of Gothic Revival design, and this is equally true of the tiles Minton produced for this and other commissions. Having broken loose from their medieval prototypes, they had become infused with the spirit of the Gothic Revival, reflecting a nineteenth-century fantasy of the Middle Ages that was inextricably linked to notions of chivalry, piety and decorative splendour. The most dramatic feature of the tiles is their use of colour, for Minton had learned to extend the polychrome effect by pressing additional coloured clays into the mould ahead of the body clay. The resulting pavements were striking, and added to the richness of the interiors of nineteenth-century churches and other Gothic Revival buildings. Pugin even went as far as to describe them as 'the best tiles in the

world . . . vastly superior to any ancient work'. Their use in church restorations, however, proved more controversial. Not only did church restoration sound the death-knell for innumerable medieval pavements whose condition had suffered from centuries of wear, but there was also growing unease about the floors that were being laid in their place. Even Sir George Gilbert Scott, who was himself known for certain excesses in his treatment of medieval buildings, was moved to decry what he described as the 'destructive inroads of *over-restoration*'. In a paper delivered at the Royal Institute of British Architects in 1862, he described the floor of the typical restored church as being:

. . . perhaps of the neatness of a Staffordshire farmer's kitchen, or, it may be, displays all the glories of encaustic tile, but the memorials to the dead have perished, and the works of Mr. Minton (to which they have fallen victims) have scornfully ousted those of his teachers, while the local patterns of old tiles have given way to those which one now finds stereotyped from one end of the country to the other . . .

Instead, he advocated the retention of any surviving medieval tiles, with new tiles to be made following their designs (fig. 5.5).

Although churches had initially been the main building type to incorporate pavements of inlaid tiles, during the second half of the century their use was to become considerably more widespread. Following the lead of the Palace of Westminster, many public buildings came to be laid with them. One of the earliest and most spectacular examples is to be found at St George's Hall in Liverpool, where a vast Minton pavement (now occasionally uncovered) was laid prior to its opening in 1854 (fig. 5.6). Many of these buildings were built in Classical rather than Gothic Revival style, and the tiles followed suit. Such tiles were even exported by Minton for use in the Capitol in Washington DC.

In addition to the developments made by Minton in the manufacture of inlaid tiles, the 1840s was a decade of technical advances which were set to have an even more profound effect on tile production. The first and most fundamental step came in 1840 with Richard Prosser's patent of a process to manufacture buttons, tesserae and other small items from compressed powdered clay. This was achieved using large screw-presses that

5.5 A tile from Salisbury Cathedral, made by the firm of Wm Godwin and dating from Gilbert Scott's restorations. Alongside is a tile from Christchurch Priory, made by the same medieval workshop that produced the original pavements at Salisbury around 1280. Gilbert Scott reputedly favoured Godwin's tiles for his ecclesiastical works. 13.1cm sq. and 14.0cm sq. V&A. C.206-1986 & 1268-1892.

5.6 St George's Hall in Liverpool. Such buildings reflect the immense civic pride of the great cities of nineteenth-century Britain. The splendid Minton pavement admirably complements the spectacular Classical Revival architecture. Courtesy of Liverpool City Council.

compacted the clay under immense pressure between metal dies (fig. 5.47). In order to manufacture tiles, the press was fitted with a fixed metal moulding box that contained the bottom die. The moulding box was filled with powdered clay, struck level, and the upper die lowered upon it by rotating the large flywheel. The tile thus formed could be ejected by means of footgear which raised the lower die from the moulding box. As the powdered clay contained only a small percentage of moisture, the tiles required considerably less time to dry than those made from plastic

clay, and the process resulted in tiles far less prone to warping. Thus a product of a consistently high quality could be achieved. The tiles were also quick to produce. Although operated by hand, as many as 1,800 6-inch tiles could be made each day on a single press. Another benefit of the technique lay in its ability to just as easily produce tiles with relief decoration by means of a specially cast die. Similarly, a pattern could be moulded onto the back of the tile, thus forming a key to help the tile bond securely with the mortar when fixed in position, and often incorporating the name or mark of the manufacturer. These back stamps are the most characteristic feature of dust-pressed tiles.

Minton was quick to see the potential of the process, and bought a share of Prosser's patent. In August 1840, production of 6-inch white-glazed tiles, buttons and tesserae began under the supervision of the engineer John Turley. Prior to this, plain tin-glazed tiles imported from the Netherlands were reputedly cheaper to buy in London than creamware or white-glazed tiles sent from Staffordshire. Nevertheless, buttons and mosaic tesserae at first accounted for the bulk of production. The virtues of the process were extolled by the architect and designer Owen Jones in 1842, in his *Designs for Mosaic Pavements*, and the technique attracted further attention in 1843 when Turley exhibited it before the Society of Arts and at a soirée of the British Association, attended by Prince Albert among other distinguished guests. The technique also attracted interest in the firm of Villeroy and Boch, who

Right: 5.8 The Centre Refreshment Room of the South Kensington Museum (now the V&A), designed by James Gamble after initial plans by Godfrey Sykes and completed in 1868–70. The wall tiles, majolica friezes and column cladding are by Minton, while the tile-mosaic floor, a classic and simple arrangement of octagonal red and smaller square black tiles, is by Maw. V&A.

Below: 5.7 A jardinière, designed by Pugin and shown at the Great Exhibition of 1851. The dust-pressed Minton tiles are early examples of the block-printing technique. Height 29.8cm. V&A. 926-1892.

5.9 The Crown Liquor Saloon in Belfast, with ceramic cladding and tile-mosaic floor by Craven Dunnill. National Trust Photographic Library. Photographer: Will Webster.

installed dust-presses at their factory at Septfontaines in Luxembourg in 1846.

The next important technical advance came in the decoration of tiles. Prior to this, transfer-printed decoration had essentially been restricted to line-engraved images printed in a single colour from copper plates. This process had been successfully used from the mid-eighteenth century to transfer printed images onto the glazed surface of tin-glazed and creamware tiles, and further developments that enabled more durable under-glaze printed decoration to be carried out had occasionally been employed in tile-making. However, the London printer Alfred Reynolds developed a process for transferring solid areas of colour to ceramics using tissue transfers printed from zinc plates which bore raised flat surfaces corresponding to the design. This block-printing process, or 'New Press' as it was called, also allowed several colours, printed successively onto the tissue from separate plates, to be transferred to the ware in one operation. Reynolds, who sought the help of Minton to perfect the process using actual ceramic pigments, jointly patented the technique with his partner F.W.M. Collins in 1848. Once again, Minton saw the potential of the process, and acquired a financial interest in the patent the following year. Though not restricted to the decoration of tiles, it was for this purpose that the process was initially used and later most extensively employed. Its first major application was in the production of large tiles designed by Pugin for the walls of the House of Commons smoking room at the Palace of Westminster, with further examples being shown at the Great Exhibition of 1851 (fig. 5.7).

Also launched by Minton at the Great Exhibition were the so-called majolica glazes developed by Léon Arnoux from 1849. The suitability of these opaque-coloured glazes for use on architectural ceramics, and in particular in conjunction with decoration modelled in high relief, resulted in various later commissions, including most notably the Royal Dairy at Windsor (fig. 4.50) and the Centre Refreshment Room and other interiors of the South Kensington Museum (fig. 5.8). These ceramic-clad rooms, which however flamboyant were conceived with practicality in mind, were the forerunners of endless hotel, railway station, and public house interiors of the later nineteenth century (fig. 5.9).

While Minton had attracted most of the attention in 1851, and had totally dominated production up until this time, the competition was to become more fierce during the second half of the century. One of the first major British competitors was Maw & Co. who, as has already been mentioned, took over the old Chamberlain & Co. tileworks at Worcester in 1850. John Hornby Maw had developed an interest in inlaid tile manufacture during the late 1840s, but had little real experience when he established the firm along with his two sons, George and Arthur. Only two years were spent at Worcester before the factory and its workforce were relocated to Broseley in Shropshire, on account of the ready availability of coal as well as clay. Tile production by T. & R. Boote Ltd of Burslem, Staffordshire, also started around 1850, and other major competitors followed with the establishment of Wm Godwin & Son at Lugwardine, Hereford, in 1861, and Malkin Edge & Co. of Burslem in 1866.

Elsewhere in Europe, the demand for floor tiles escalated from the 1860s, and the technical developments pioneered in Britain began to take hold, particularly in Germany, Belgium and France. Villeroy and Boch, who established a floor tile manufactory at Mettlach in 1866, were the market leaders in Germany and the Netherlands. In 1868 the *Art Journal* commented that 'their factories are extensive,

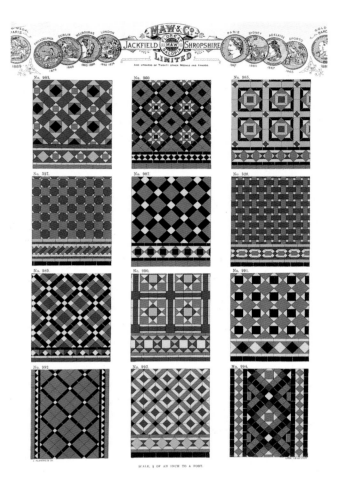

5.10 A range of simple tile-mosaic patterns as offered by Maw & Co. in a catalogue of around 1890. V&A (National Art Library).

employing, we understand, two or three thousand workmen: a very large number of these are engaged in making encaustic tiles for the floors of churches, halls &c.' The Belgian manufacturer Boch Frères also entered the market, establishing a factory primarily for the production of floor tiles at Maubeuge in France in 1861. Under Victor Regnauld's directorship of the great French porcelain factory of Sèvres (1852–70), a department was established for the development of architectural and garden wares. Tiles decorated with richly coloured opaque glazes and following Moorish designs were shown by Sèvres at the Paris Exposition Universelle of 1867, alongside the tilework of other French and British manufacturers. A report on this exhibition for the *Art Journal* demonstrated the wide range of products now on offer from Maw & Co., who showed 'tiles for ordinary uses, encaustic tiles of various colours, "figured" glazed tiles, and majolica embossed, for wall linings, dados, fireplace linings, &c'. These were, they glowingly stated, 'in all cases . . . examples of pure Art'.

Though the range of tiles was clearly increasing, the bulk of the output of the industry was still paving tiles, with both inlaid and geometrical mosaic tiles being produced. Despite being specially shaped to fit the sometimes complex arrangements advertised in company catalogues, these mosaic tiles, each of a single colour of clay, could be relatively easily made using the dust-pressing technique. In 1863, however, the engineers William Boulton and Joseph Worthington patented a process that for the first time allowed inlaid tiles to be made in this way. Dust-presses for inlaid tiles were similar to standard types, except that the moulding box in which the tiles were formed could be raised or lowered, or moved out from under the line of the press. With the box in this latter position, and lowered so that the bottom die stood proud, the inlay was first pressed by hand onto the die using a brass template and correspondingly shaped pressing plate. The moulding box was then raised around the bottom die, and filled with sufficient dust clay to form the body of the tile. The box was then slid under the press and the clay compacted. Though dust-pressed inlaid tiles were produced by firms such as T. & R. Boote and Malkin Edge, the technique did not altogether replace their manufacture with plastic clay, which Minton and others continued to practise. That the demand for decorated floor tiles was so great was a consequence of their increasingly widespread use. In addition to churches and public buildings, inlaid and mosaic tiles had by the mid-1860s become a typical feature of the aspiring middle-class home. Charles Eastlake's *Hints on Household Taste*, which in 1868 was the first of an endless succession of instructive household manuals, promoted the use of floor tiles without qualification:

There can be little doubt that the best mode of treating a hall-floor, whether in town or country, is to pave it with encaustic tiles. This branch of art-manufacture is one of the most hopeful, in regard to taste, now carried on in this country. It has not only reached great technical perfection as far as material and colour are concerned, but, aided by the designs supplied by many architects of acknowledged skill, it has gradually become a means of decoration which, for beauty of effect, durability, and cheapness, has scarcely a parallel.

This use of geometrical mosaic tiles for hall floors, the front pathways of villas and terraced houses, and elsewhere in the home where a durable and hygienic surface was required, continued in popularity through to the Edwardian period (fig. 5.10). The choice of designs would be determined by the affluence of the householder and the

5.11 A panel of tiles illustrating the story of 'Sleeping Beauty', designed by Edward Burne-Jones, with 'Swan' border tiles designed by Morris. The panel is one of three made by Morris, Marshall, Faulkner & Co. around 1864–5 as overmantels for bedrooms in the house of the painter Myles Birket Foster, The Hill, at Witley, Surrey. Width 121cm. V&A. Circ.520-1973.

situation in which the tiles were to be used, and ranged from the simplest geometrical arrangements through to complex and splendid designs which might incorporate both inlaid and mosaic tiles.

In counterpoint to the seemingly unstoppable process of industrialisation, by the 1860s new forces were coming into play in the fields of architecture and design. Of particular influence was William Morris, founder in 1861 of the decorators and retailers Morris, Marshall, Faulkner & Co. The products of the firm ranged from stained glass for churches through to furniture, textiles, table-glass and wallpaper, all executed in celebration of the virtues of hand craftsmanship. As early as 1862, tiles were also produced,

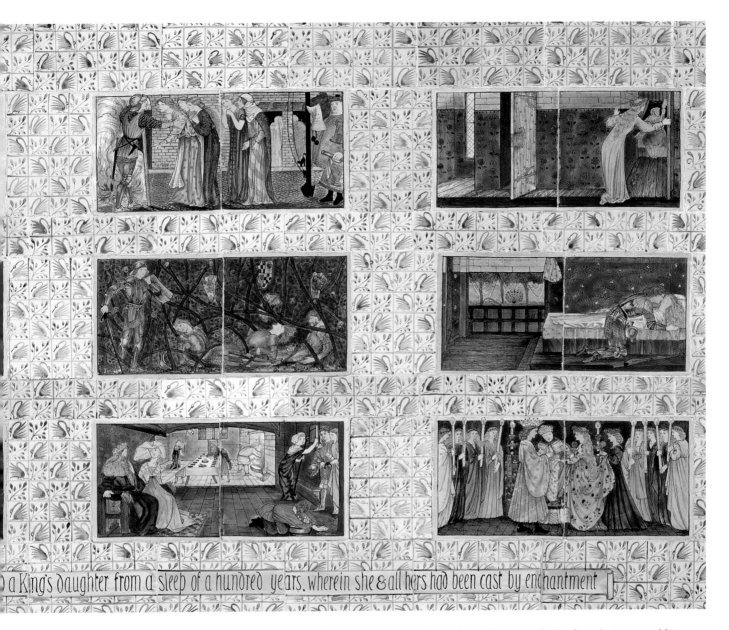

a King's daughter from a sleep of a hundred years, wherein she & all hers had been cast by enchantment

and the company accounts record the importance of sales of the article. Morris's tiles were painted onto white tin-glazed blanks supplied from Holland, and fired alongside stained glass in a kiln designed for that purpose. The results were at best patchy, yet the designs were extraordinary, with simple repeating motifs being used alongside small figurative panels that call to mind medieval manuscript illuminations (fig. 5.11). Perhaps owing to the technical difficulties, from the mid-1870s Morris pressed several Dutch firms, including Ravesteijn of Utrecht, into the production of his designs. Morris's excursions into the world of tile design and manufacture have frequently been seen simply as a reaction to industrial production. However, there can have been few decorated wall tiles on

the market when Morris made his first designs, and his motivation should perhaps more appropriately be seen as part of the growing interest among architects and designers in vernacular British architecture and decorative art of the seventeenth and eighteenth centuries.

Principal among the exponents of the vernacular was the architect Richard Norman Shaw, who helped to pioneer the 'Old English' and 'Queen Anne' styles. Hand-painted tiles featured regularly in such interiors. Often they were set in fireplaces (fig. 5.12), but at Cragside in Northumberland, one of Shaw's finest houses, a cold bath was lined with Dutch painted tin-glazed tiles to great effect (fig. 5.13). Such tiles were rooted in a tradition established in the seventeenth and eighteenth centuries with resonance both

Left: 5.12 The Oak Room at Wightwick Manor, near Wolverhampton (1887–93). Designed by Edward Ould in the 'Old English' style, Wightwick has interiors rich in Arts and Crafts furnishings. The hand-painted Dutch tiles copy Iznik patterns and were from a range supplied by Thomas Elsley. National Trust Photographic Library. Photographer: Andreas von Einsiedel.

Above: 5.13 The Turkish baths at Cragside in Northumberland (1869–85), one of Richard Norman Shaw's most adventurous country house schemes. The baths were constructed in 1870. National Trust Photographic Library. Photographer: Andreas von Einsiedel.

Left: 5.14 A tile painted with boxing hares in ruby lustre, made by the firm of Wm De Morgan at Chelsea. An industrially produced blank has been used. 15.2cm sq. V&A. Circ.118-1915.

in the Netherlands and in England – a condition to which Morris's own tiles certainly aspired. Shaw also played a major role in the design of the garden suburb of Bedford Park in London, which included among its buildings The Tabard Inn and Stores. Built in 1879–80, the interior of the public house was, and still remains, lined with hand-painted tiles produced by the firm of William De Morgan.

An associate of Morris, with whom he sometimes collaborated in the production of tiles, William De Morgan became the leading pottery and tile manufacturer associated with the Arts and Crafts movement. Ever the experimenter, De Morgan set fire to his parents' house in 1871 while attempting to produce lustreware from a kiln in the cellar. Establishing himself at Cheyne Row in Chelsea the following year, he there perfected the lustre technique (fig. 5.14) and developed a range of under-glaze 'Persian' colours (primarily blue, turquoise and green) which were in fact closer to the palette of Syrian tiles (figs 5.41 and 5.42). At Chelsea, De Morgan took on a number of assistants to decorate his tiles, initially buying in industrially produced dust-pressed blanks, but from 1876 using his own hand-made tiles. In 1882, the workshop moved to Merton Abbey, and then in 1889 to Fulham, where De Morgan was in partnership with the architect Halsey Ricardo. De Morgan's technique for transferring the patterns to the tiles was unusual. Rather than pouncing the design, the decoration was painted onto a sheet of fine tissue placed on a sheet of glass, behind which an outline of the pattern acted as a guide. The tissue was then placed face-down on the slip-coated surface of the tile and covered with clear glaze. During the firing the tissue would burn away. Though the De Morgan pottery was not a great commercial success, his tiles became a typical feature of Aesthetic Movement, Arts and Crafts, and Moorish interiors, finding particular application in fireplaces and domestic furniture (fig. 5.15), but also in the grander schemes of the houses of wealthy patrons and the smoking rooms of P&O liners.

In the major industries, however, the shifts in production that had begun to take place before 1870 became compounded in the final decades of the century, and a vast array of wall tiles appeared on the market alongside the already well-established ranges of floor tiles. With the necessary technical advances already long in place, the development of this market ran in parallel to the introduction of a variety of new or modified applications for tilework. In the home, modifications to the design of cast-iron fire-grates brought tiles to prominence. In order to improve efficiency, the

standard late nineteenth-century grate had a narrow vertical opening with a canopy hood and splayed tiled cheeks, the tiles being fixed to metal plates that bolted onto the frame (fig. 5.16). The design of the grates thus made the tiles an obligatory feature, though one that could be mixed and matched according to taste. It was largely in conjunction with these fireplaces that the vast ranges of pictorial tile series of the later nineteenth century were developed (fig. 5.17). Hearths were also usually tiled, and for these, sturdier tiles were employed. Often decorated with simple block-printed patterns, these formed something of an intermediate type between floor and wall tiles (fig. 5.18). Extensive tiling was also to be found in bathrooms, which began to appear in more affluent homes following the arrival of running water in the 1870s (figs 5.19 and 5.20), and in the common areas of apartment blocks, including most notably the tenement closes of Glasgow and Edinburgh. Tiled porches also became

5.15 A Liberty & Co. oak washstand, designed in 1894 and set with 'Nine Square' and plain tiles by De Morgan. V&A. W.18-1984.

Left: 5.16 The bedroom of 'The Tenement House' in Glasgow. The all-in-one cast-iron fireplace is of typical late-Victorian form with angled cheeks set with tiles. The National Trust for Scotland.

5.17 Block-printed tiles from the 'Shakespeare' series, designed by John Moyr Smith for Minton's China Works. Width 15.2cm. V&A. C.14&15-1971

popular. All these developments were compounded by the boom in domestic building.

Meanwhile, attempts to improve the standard of public health resulted in the construction of numerous public baths and swimming pools, while the increased awareness of hygiene also encouraged the use of tiling in hospitals (fig. 5.21). The growth of food retailing, coupled again with demand for cleanliness, led manufacturers to offer standard tiling schemes for shop interiors, these typically incorporating pictorial panels or friezes set alongside plain tiles, while larger retailers might commission their own schemes (fig. 5.22). Other new building types, such as underground stations, also furthered the demand. Typical of many of these extensive tiling schemes is their use of bright, transparent, coloured glazes which gained in popularity over the opaque majolica type.

To meet the increased demand, new manufacturers were

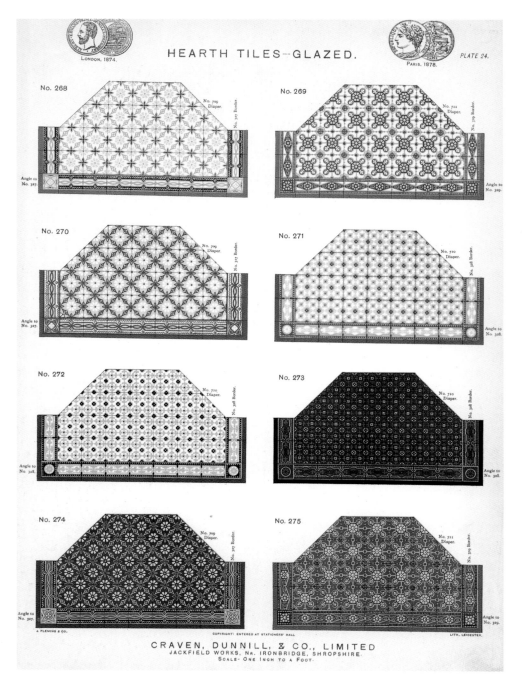

HEARTH TILES—GLAZED.   PLATE 24.

No. 268   No. 269
No. 270   No. 271
No. 272   No. 273
No. 274   No. 275

CRAVEN, DUNNILL, & CO., LIMITED
JACKFIELD WORKS, NR. IRONBRIDGE, SHROPSHIRE.
SCALE—ONE INCH TO A FOOT.

5.18 Designs for hearth tiling by Craven Dunnill from a catalogue of 1879. V&A (National Art Library).

established, and new purpose-built factories constructed (see pp148–9). The first of these was the revolutionary new tileworks built in 1868–9 for Michael Daintry Hollins, the direct result of the dissolution of his partnership with Colin Minton Campbell and the break-up of the Minton firm. Hollins and Campbell had become partners of Herbert Minton in 1845 and 1849 respectively, and since Minton's death in 1858 had continued the running of the firm, with Hollins in charge of tile production. Following the split in 1868, Hollins retained the tile business and the name Minton, Hollins & Co., and used capital raised from the settlement to finance the new works. Campbell, meanwhile, took the rest of the business and began trading as Minton's China Works. He produced wall tiles, and also gained an interest in floor tile manufacture from 1875 when he took over the business of another former Minton partner, Robert Minton Taylor. This firm came to trade as the Campbell Tile Co. With the benefits of art education and training in mind, Campbell also founded Minton's Art Pottery Studio in South Kensington in 1871. A variety of

5.19 A bathroom scheme in London manufacturer Doulton & Co.'s 1904 catalogue for the French market. Writing in Germany in the same year, Hermann Muthesius described Doulton's catalogues as 'the best guide to the present state of development of the bathroom'. V&A (National Art Library).

5.20 A typical tiling scheme as illustrated in a Doulton & Co. catalogue of 1898. The floor is covered with mosaic tiles, while the walls are tiled in bands, with the dado, upper wall and frieze receiving different treatments. V&A.

notable designers and illustrators, including Henry Stacy Marks, William Wise and John Moyr Smith, became associated with Minton's during this period, supplying designs to both the London studio and for mass production at Stoke (figs 5.17 and 5.23). Meanwhile, prominent designers such as Walter Crane and Lewis Day also turned their attention to tiles on occasion, both working for Maw's and later for Pilkington's Tile & Pottery Co. in Lancashire (fig. 5.24). Expanding production at Maw's led to their relocation to Jackfield in 1883, close to the works established by Craven Dunnill & Co. in 1872 (now the Jackfield Tile Museum). Among other newcomers to the industry around this time was J.C. Edwards of Ruabon in Wales, while established pottery manufacturers such as Doulton & Co., Josiah Wedgwood & Sons and W.T. Copeland & Sons also revived or initiated tile production. Small-scale firms such as London decorators W.B Simpson & Sons also responded to the demand for

tiled interiors and produced hand-painted panels using industrially made blanks (fig. 5.25).

The demand for tiles of all types grew across Europe from the 1870s. Wall and floor tiles were made in quantity by Villeroy and Boch at Mettlach, Dresden and Merzig, and by Boch Frères at Maubeuge and La Louviére. In France, Hippolyte Boulenger & Cie of Choisy-le-Roi became a leading manufacturer of wall tiles and other architectural ceramics, producing many finely painted pictorial panels (fig. 5.26). The Parisian manufacturers Jules Loebnitz, Emile Muller and Alexandre Bigot, along with Charles Gréber of Beauvais, instead concentrated on more richly ornamented, glazed architectural stonewares and terracottas, these frequently being applied to building façades. Bigot, in particular, became associated with the pioneers of the art nouveau style. Large stoneware tiles with abstract decoration in high relief provided a principal component in the decoration of the entrance hall of Hector Guimard's *Le Castel Béranger* of 1894–8. In the Beauvais region, the Boulenger factory at Auneuil, built in 1883,

Above: 5.21 'Mary, Mary, Quite Contrary' by Margaret Thompson at Doulton's for a children's ward at University College Hospital, London. According to a booklet published by the pottery in 1904, the panels served to 'brighten and cheer the enforced stay of the weary sufferers in the wards, and to bring fresh thoughts of nature and happiness to their tired minds'. Height 114cm. V&A. C.112-1977.

Right: 5.22 Harrods' food hall in London, with tiles made by Doulton's and installed in 1902. The pictorial panels were designed by William J. Neatby. Royal Institute of British Architects.

Above: 5.23 A transfer-printed tile from a series depicting 'Animals on the Farm', designed by William Wise for Minton's China Works after an etching by Robert Hills, around 1879. 15.2cm sq. V&A. C.14-1986.

Left: 5.24 'Flora's Train', designed by Walter Crane for Pilkington's in 1900–1. The style blends Victorian book illustration with art nouveau. The outlines of the patterns have been pressed in relief, in imitation of tube-lining. Each 15.2cm sq. V&A. 309 to E-1903.

became a major producer of inlaid floor tiles. Meanwhile, the French architect and ceramicist Léon Parvillée is noteworthy for his reproductions of tiles for building restorations (fig. 3.18). His slip-decorated versions of medieval inlaid tiles were put to use by the Gothic Revival architect Viollet-le-Duc.

In Holland, Spain and Portugal, where the production of hand-made tin-glazed tiles had continued in an unbroken tradition, the adoption of new production techniques was more gradual. Nevertheless, by the late nineteenth century, dust-pressed tiles were made in Delft by the long-established firm of De Porceleyne Fles, and by new firms such as Rozenburg in The Hague and De Distel in Amsterdam. In Portugal, a large demand for tilework ensued as the country emerged from the political and economic crisis of the earlier part of the century. Here, a fashion emerged for covering entire building façades with tiles. Traditional techniques were maintained, although factories such as Sacavém in Lisbon produced relief-decorated tiles using the new production methods.

Spanish tile-making had been represented in the 1851 exhibition by the products of the Valencian factory of Rafael González Valls. Despite continuing in the tin-glazed tradition, the firm had nevertheless recently pioneered the use of stencilling alongside more traditional painted decoration. Among the designs shown were examples reflecting the growing stylistic eclecticism of the century, with Moorish geometrical patterns being given contemporary treatments. Others reflected the lingering neo-classicism typical of the tilework of Valéncia and Onda

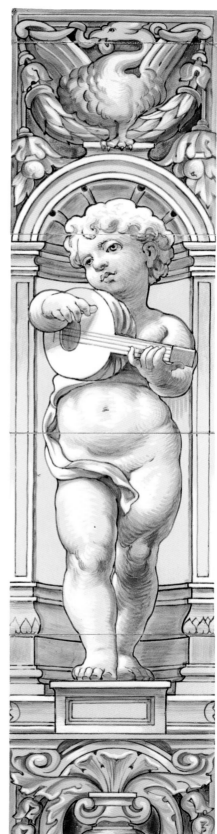

5.25 A panel of tiles painted by A.S. Coke at W.B. Simpson & Sons around 1873 for the decorations of The Criterion, a 'gastronomic temple' with dining rooms, grand hall and theatre, in Piccadilly, London. Width 22.9cm. V&A. C.80-1969.

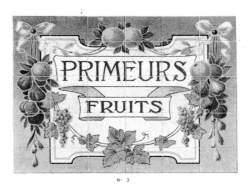

5.26 A range of tile panels for shops, offered by Hippolyte Boulenger & Cie in their 1921 catalogue. Many of the designs have a lingering art nouveau feel. V&A (National Art Library).

5.27 One of twenty-two frames of tiles shown at the Great Exhibition by the firm of Rafael González Valls of Valencia. Each 20.2cm sq. V&A. C.94-1998.

Above right: 5.28 The serpentine benches of Gaudí's Park Güell in Barcelona, constructed between 1900 and 1914. © Bastin & Evrard – Brussels.

Right: 5.29 The Majolika Haus, a residential block in Vienna, designed by Otto Wagner in 1898. Royal Institute of British Architects.

(fig. 5.27). Dust-pressing was practised by a handful of manufacturers in Spain from the mid-nineteenth century. Miguel Nolla, for example, used the technique to produce mosaic tesserae at his factory in Valéncia from 1860, and Juan Bautista White y Boneli introduced it for the manufacture of tiles in the same year. Nevertheless it was not to become widespread until the end of the century. There was, however, a revival of the tile industry in the later part of the century, with manufacturers frequently producing tiles based on historical prototypes. In Seville, this had occurred following the introduction of tile manufacture at Pickman y Cía sometime around 1870. Painted and lustred tiles, and others based on earlier *arista* types, were made by Pickman and others, including Mensaque Hermanos y Cía and Ramos Rejano. Production in Catalonia underwent a similar revival at the hands of manufacturers such as Pujol y Bausis. Catalonian tilework, however, perhaps achieved its greatest degree of expression at the hands of the architect Antoní Gaudí. Standard mass-produced tiles and other ceramic items were given an extraordinary treatment, being fragmented and applied as mosaic to curving organic surfaces, frequently suggestive of reptilian forms. Gaudí's most complete manifestations of this technique can be found in the architectural features of Park Güell, constructed between 1900 and 1914, and in contemporary buildings such as the Casa Batlló (fig. 5.28).

In central Europe, tile production was dominated by the firms of Rako in the Czech Republic and Zsolnay of Pécs in Hungary. Among the products of Zsolnay was a frost-resistant stoneware termed Pyrogranit that provided a robust medium for architectural decoration. Richly glazed Pyrogranit tiles were used extensively by architects such as Ödön Lechner, a pioneer of Hungarian art nouveau, who through buildings such as the Museum of Applied Arts in Budapest (1896) sought to create a distinctive national architectural style. In Austria, tilework was also on occasion employed by the architects of the Secession. The entire façade of Otto Wagner's Majolika Haus in Vienna, built in 1898, is clad with tiles that form across their surface an ornate network of curvilinear tendrils, foliage and flowers (fig. 5.29).

From the turn of the century, tile manufacturers throughout Europe responded increasingly to the growing popularity of art nouveau. Following the Paris *Exposition Universelle* of 1900, Pilkington's Tile and Pottery Co. commissioned designs from Alfonse Mucha, and the hand-painted figurative panels that resulted were shown at Glasgow in 1901. Under the directorship of Léon Victor Solon (1900–9), Minton's China Works produced finely

decorated figurative and ornamental panels in the tube-lining technique to designs by Solon or his assistant John Wadsworth. The technique proved well suited to the sinuous motifs of art nouveau, with fluid lines of clay slip delineating patterns which were filled in with coloured glazes. Tube-lined decoration was widely reproduced by moulding the raised outlines of the designs – a technique analogous with the *arista* tiles of Spain (fig. 5.24). Many mass-produced tiles were fairly lukewarm imitations of the art nouveau style. More forward-looking, however, were the floor tiles produced by Villeroy and Boch in Mettlach to designs by the architect and industrial designer Peter Behrens (fig. 5.30). Produced following Behrens' appointment as director of the *Kunstgewerbeschule* in Düsseldorf in 1903, their taut geometrical patterns represented a move away from art nouveau towards a new vocabulary of precise abstract forms. Such tiles were used in his scheme for the Jungbrunnen restaurant at the *Kunst-*

Above: 5.30 An inlaid floor tile, designed by Peter Behrens for Villeroy and Boch. 15.0cm sq. V&A. C.25-1998.

Left: 5.31 'The Exmouth' fireplace by Candy and Co. of Newton Abbot, Devon. A typical slabbed briquette and tile fireplace, which came supplied in pre-formed sections for easy fixing. V&A (National Art Library).

Right: 5.32 The tiled entrance hall of Highpoint No.2 (1935–8), a modernist residential block at Highgate, London, designed by Berthold Lubetkin/Tecton. The illustration was included in the *Architectural Review*'s survey of tiles in May 1939. Royal Institute of British Architects.

und-Gartenbau-Ausstellung held in Düsseldorf in 1904.

While the popularity of art nouveau helped to sustain demand for decorative tiles during the first decade of the twentieth century, their use seems to have increasingly been at odds with progressive taste. Even in the interior schemes offered by the London retailer Liberty & Co., who were closely associated with the movement, there was a preference for tiles of plain colours (fig. 5.15). Similar plain tiling was to be found in the fireplaces of the vernacular 'cottage' interiors offered by rivals Heals. In the new suburban houses of Edwardian Britain, these models seem to have influenced the standard types, with fireplace surrounds being constructed from tiles (sometimes specially shaped) of a single colour. Of a series of fireplaces installed in Hampstead around 1904, Ambrose Wood recorded the colours used as being 'chiefly crimson, old gold, golden-yellow, cream, light-green, shrimp-pink, and a rich deep tint of blue'. These fireplaces were finished with wooden overmantels. The more constructional use of tiles in such fireplaces, with tilework increasingly replacing elements of the cast-iron grate, makes them the forerunners of the 'slabbed-up' tile fireplaces that became standard from the 1930s (fig. 5.31).

In the interwar period, the functional characteristics of tilework continued to be exploited. Its application tended to be in areas where these were fully realised, such as fireplaces, kitchens, and bathrooms, as well as public spaces and building façades. Its use tended to be more architectural, creating large surfaces of white, cream or soft, often mottled, colour. Decorated tiles, if used at all, might provide accents of colour or occasional motifs within an otherwise plain scheme. As functionalism became a tenet of the architects and designers of the Modern Movement, so the practical aspects of tilework were utilised within their schemes. Thus cheap ceramic tiles were put into service in Grete Schütte-Lihotzky's masterpiece of standardisation and rationalism, the *Frankfurter Küche* (Frankfurt Kitchen), designed in 1926, and used within the social housing programmes of the city, while at the other end of the Modernist spectrum, tiles provided a tight-fitting skin which protected but left visible the stylish architectural forms of Tecton's Highpoint No.2 (fig. 5.32). During this period, architectural ceramic cladding moved towards the conventions of tilework, with a preference for flat surfaces and shallow mouldings replacing the earlier practices of using terracotta in imitation of structural masonry and ornamental carving. The cinemas of the 1930s were particularly notable for their matt-glazed ceramic façades (frequently of Doulton's

Carraraware), which admirably complemented their glamorous American-influenced Moderne architecture (fig. 5.33).

The use of pattern on tiles was not, however, altogether extinguished. The virtues of hand-decorated furnishings had earlier been espoused by the artist and critic Roger Fry, whose Omega Workshops produced painted tin-glazed fireplace tiles from 1914 (see pp150–1). The pioneer studio potter, Bernard Leach, also began production of hand-made and decorated stoneware tiles at St Ives around 1927. These proved the perfect vehicle for Leach's fluid brushwork, the designs exhibiting both English medieval and Japanese influences (fig. 5.34). On a somewhat larger scale, hand-painted tin-glazed tiles were being produced by Carter & Co. by 1920. These were designed by a range of highly competent in-house staff as well as freelance artists such as Edward Bawden (fig. 5.35). Carter's, who had taken over the Architectural Pottery Co. of Poole, Dorset, in 1895, were by this time one of Britain's leading producers of tiles and architectural ceramics. In southern Europe, however, the traditions of painted tilework remained strong. In Seville, the tile decorations of the Plaza de España and other buildings of the 1929 *Exposición Iberoamericana* marked a high point in production.

Considerable advances in production technologies and factory organisation took place during the course of the twentieth century. In 1913, Carter's followed J.H. Barrett & Co. to become the second tileworks in England to install a continuously fired Dressler tunnel-kiln. Although the first Dressler at Carter's was plagued with technical problems, the tunnel-kiln came to revolutionise production. A 310ft gas-fired tunnel-kiln and its associated 200ft drying tunnel, installed at Carter's in the mid-1960s, could handle over twelve million tiles each year. The tiles, produced on semi- or fully automatic presses, were packed in saggars and loaded onto kiln cars that ran on rails through the drying tunnel and kiln, undergoing a carefully controlled sequence of temperature changes in the process. Improvements in firing technologies in the post-war period were matched by advances in the clay body, enabling thinner tiles to be produced, as well as in the conformity of glazes to standard colours. In addition, other innovations such as moulded lugs on the edges of tiles to ensure accurate spacing were introduced. The industry in Britain also underwent a period of concentration. By the early 1960s, four firms alone dominated the market: Richards Tiles Ltd, H. & R.

5.33 Architectural ceramics used to dramatic effect on the façade of the Odeon, Sutton Coldfield. Royal Institute of British Architects.

Left: 5.34 Hand-painted stoneware tiles, made by Bernard Leach in 1938. Leach described his tiles as having 'a certain degree of irregularity for which no apology is needed'. One of the tiles shows the wood-burning climbing kiln built by Leach and Hamada Shoji at St Ives. Each 15.0cm sq. V&A. C.47-1946.

Right: 5.35 The 'Sporting' series of hand-painted tin-glazed tiles, designed by Edward Bawden for Carter & Co. around 1921–5. Typical of Bawden's work of the period, the designs offer an affectionate portrayal of British life. Each 12.7cm sq. V&A. C.11-1978.

Johnson Ltd, Pilkington's and Carter's. The formation of H. & R. Johnson-Richards Ltd in 1968, along with Pilkington's takeover of Carter's in 1964, effectively reduced this to two. Minton Hollins & Co. and the Campbell Tile Co., the two branches of the Minton firm that continued tile production into the 1960s, were both subsumed by Johnson-Richards.

Of the British firms, Carter's was the acknowledged design leader. The major post-war development in tile decoration, that of silk-screen printing, was pioneered there by Reginald Till along with the designer Peggy Angus. The use of silk-screen printed 'pattern-building' tiles to build up strong abstract designs over large surfaces was particularly successful, and continued the more architectural approaches to tilework favoured in the interwar period (fig. 5.36). The use of tilework to form lively and colourful decorative surfaces within architectural

settings also resulted in the widespread post-war phenomenon of the tile mural. Typically deployed in public spaces, within supermarkets or on building façades, the medium has often submitted itself to didactic or even propagandist treatments, and frequently benefited from the strongly graphic qualities of 1950s and 1960s art and design (fig. 5.37). Tiled murals maintained their popularity into the 1970s, and a revival of interest in this form of decoration has occurred in recent years. Its production has led to collaborations between artists and designers and the tile industry, and has also provided opportunities for the growing range of small independent workshops and craft potters to work on a larger scale. These craftsmen and women, of whom the Sussex-based potters Kenneth Clark and Ann Wynn Reeves are notable examples, have helped to ensure that original and experimental tile decoration has continued to be produced (fig. 5.38). The somewhat closer

Left: 5.36 The Carter stand at the 1951 Building Trades Exhibition, designed by F.R.S. Yorke and incorporating screen-printed tiles designed by Peggy Angus. V&A.

Right: 5.37 A tile mural on the Avenida Infante Santo in Lisbon, designed by Muria Keil for the Viúva Lamego factory and made in 1959. Keil went on to design a number of panels for stations on Lisbon's Metro. Courtesy of Hirmer Verlag, Munich.

relationship of artists and industry that exists in parts of Scandinavia has, meanwhile, led to imaginative tilework such as that produced by Rut Bryk for Arabia in Finland (fig. 5.39).

The way in which tiles are used in today's homes reflects a diversity of attitudes and approaches. Fireplaces, largely stripped of their practical function, have become decorative and symbolic, reflecting a nostalgic vision of cosy homeliness. The cast-iron grates of the Victorian and Edwardian periods, ripped from buildings in the 1960s and 1970s, are now being lovingly returned. This might reflect a wider concern for period detail and for cultural and domestic heritage, yet the almost complete obliteration of the slabbed-up fireplaces of the mid-twentieth century has so far passed in marked silence. The demand for 'heritage' tiles, which range from debased versions of period designs through to high-quality reproductions using original techniques, reflects the popularity of certain styles of decoration, but perhaps does little to further contemporary design. Tiles are, of course, more prevalent in the functional settings of the bathroom and kitchen, and it is the challenge of designing for these locations that has resulted in the greatest degree of creativity. Perhaps inevitably, the most innovative products have originated

a non-slip surface. Good design sense has been combined with wit and humour to produce tiles that are both functional but also beautiful. Similarly well-conceived are Dominic Crinson's tiles for use in kitchens and bathrooms, which employ computer-imaging techniques in the reproduction of their decoration (fig. 5.40). Colourful and stylish, the tiles are decorated with designs entirely appropriate to their intended setting. Such examples serve to demonstrate that, with the application of new technologies or by innovative approaches to design, there is still the potential for new developments in this age-old medium. Practical, durable, ceramic tilework with strikingly modern decoration would seem to have a continuing appeal.

Left: 5.38 Hand- silk-screen-printed tiles, designed by Ann Wynn Reeves and made by the Kenneth Clark Pottery. Industrially produced tile blanks have been used. V&A. C.158 to C-1980.

Opposite: 5.39 A panel of tiles made by Rut Bryk for the firm of Arabia, Helsinki, Finland, around 1960. The decoration is rich and tapestry-like, yet demonstrates

the artist's increasing interest in geometrical relief patterning. 48cm sq. V&A. Circ.101-1963.

Below: 5.40 Kitchen tiles from a series of fruit and vegetable designs, produced using computer-imaging techniques by Dominic Crinson in London. The designs are wholly appropriate to their setting, cut fruit and vegetables being *exactly* what you find in a kitchen.

outside the major industries. A superb example can be found in the 'Glassdrop' bathroom floor tiles designed by Arnoud Visser in 1997 for the Dutch consortium Droog. Beads of splashed water are replicated on the surface of these tiles, the relief effect of which (paradoxically) creates

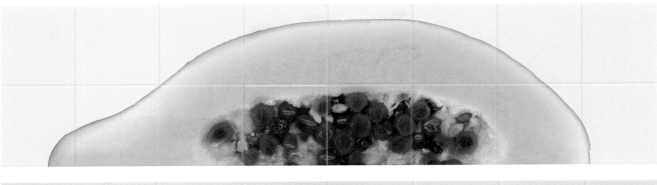

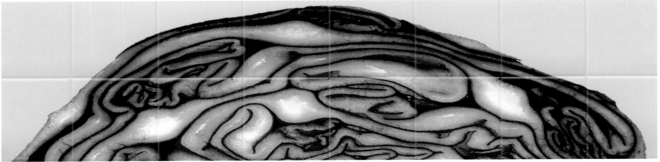

Islamic Influences

Left: 5.41 The Arab Hall in Leighton House, built in 1877–9 and incorporating a wealth of Islamic tilework, primarily from Syria. The glass mosaic frieze above the tile panels was designed by Walter Crane. The Royal Borough of Kensington and Chelsea, Leighton House Museum.

Above: 5.42 A watercolour design for a tile panel decorated with 'Persian' foliage, made by William de Morgan, probably around 1882–8. Height. 99.2cm. V&A. E.422-1917.

The pottery and tilework of the Islamic world became a source of fascination for collectors, aesthetes, designers and ceramicists during the nineteenth century. Travel to the Levant had become a fashionable variation of the Grand Tour, and considerable quantities of antique and contemporary tiles were brought from Syria, Turkey and Iran for sale on the European market. The tilework of Moorish Spain also attracted interest, fuelled by Owen Jones' publication of designs from the Alhambra and the construction of the Alhambra Court at the re-erected Crystal Palace in 1854. Moorish and other Islamic designs quickly became part of the repertoire of British tile

manufacturers, and both Minton and Maw exhibited ceramics and tiles of Moorish style at the London 1862 Exhibition.

Other ceramicists, including William Burton (of Pilkington's) and William De Morgan, became as fascinated with the production techniques of the Islamic potters as they were with the decoration of the wares, and experimented endlessly to reproduce their effects. De Morgan succeeded in reinventing the Islamic lustre technique, and produced numerous tile and pottery designs in the 'Persian' style ('Persian' being used as something of a catch-all to describe the various Islamic wares). One of De Morgan's greatest achievements lay in his

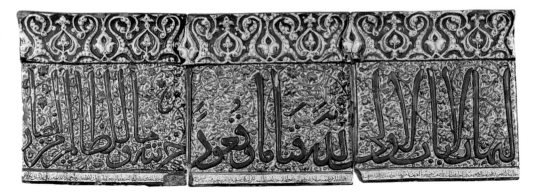

5.43 Fragments of a frieze of lustre tiles, made at Kashan in Iran around 1200–15. The tiles are part of a large group collected between 1873 and 1885 by the director of the Persian Telegraph Department, Robert Murdoch Smith, on behalf of the South Kensington Museum (now the V&A). Many such tiles were acquired by travellers using both legitimate as well as less scrupulous means. Height 43.8cm. V&A. 1481-1876.

5.44 A panel of tiles made at Isnik in Turkey around 1550–1600, decorated in typically formal style and employing a characteristic intense red, applied as a thick iron-rich slip. Height. 59cm. V&A. 428-1900.

involvement with the creation of the Arab Hall at the painter Frederic Leighton's house in Kensington. Built in 1877–9 by George Aitchison, the Arab Hall is perhaps the most complete expression of a nineteenth-century fantasy of a Moorish interior ever realised. Based on the architecture of La Zisa, a palace in Palermo in Sicily, it provided the setting for Leighton's superb collection of sixteenth- and seventeenth-century Syrian and Turkish tiles. These were laid out by De Morgan, who also utilised his technical skills to manufacture reproductions where gaps were present in the designs.

Interiors in a wide range of late nineteenth-century buildings were also decorated with tiling schemes inspired, however loosely, by Moorish and Islamic art and architecture. The Moorish style became particularly associated with places of entertainment and relaxation, and hotels, theatres, public houses and even the smoking rooms of ocean liners all received the treatment. Turkish baths – then becoming increasingly fashionable – were invariably decorated in this manner, their popularity reflecting the public fascination with all that was perceived as exotic.

A Nineteenth-Century Tile Factory

Although some of Staffordshire's ceramic factories (or 'pot-banks') of the mid-nineteenth century had spacious and well-ventilated workshops, the majority afforded appalling conditions to their staff, who worked in cramped and squalid buildings, exposed to a variety of toxic materials and extremes of heat. Many factories, having responded to the demands of increased production by expanding in a piecemeal fashion, were made up of ramshackle conglomerations of buildings.

However, factory legislation of 1864 improved the conditions of pottery workers, reducing the number of hours worked and restricting the use of child labour. The resultant lack of unskilled labour encouraged greater and more efficient organisation, as well as an increase in the use of machinery and steam-power, which had hitherto been restricted to the clay preparation areas of larger factories. Greater consideration was also paid to factory design. Though the traditional arrangement of working buildings around a central courtyard remained the most popular, the new and rational linear plan was developed in the 1860s, with tileworks leading the way.

The first of these was the new purpose-built tile factory of Minton Hollins & Co. in Stoke-on-Trent, designed by Charles Lynam and constructed in 1868–9. This was organised as a series

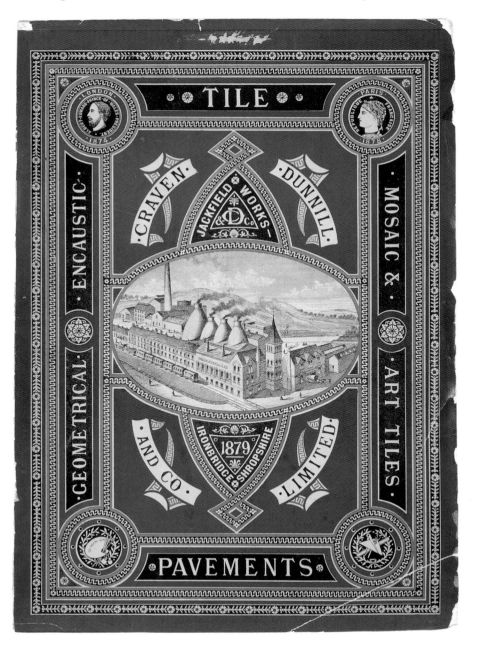

Left: 5.45 The new Craven Dunnill works, proudly shown on the cover of their 1879 catalogue. At the far left, on either side of a central driveway, are the clay preparation and storage areas. These are followed by workshops, bottle ovens, and finally the offices, studios and showrooms of the grand entrance block. V&A (National Art Library).

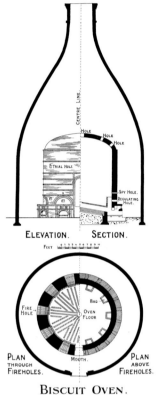

ELEVATION. SECTION.

PLAN THROUGH FIREHOLES. PLAN ABOVE FIREHOLES.

BISCUIT OVEN.
W. Campbell, Architect, Hanley.

Above: 5.48 Tile dippers glazing tiles at Carter & Co., Poole, before 1904. One of the industry's more hazardous occupations, the use of lead glazes resulted in numerous cases of poisoning. The 1864 legislation stipulated that no child, young person or woman was to be allowed to eat in the dipping room. V&A.

Top right: 5.46 A typical bottle oven: a domed kiln is set within the classic bottle-shaped structure or 'hovel'. Separate kilns

were used for the initial 'biscuit' firing, and where appropriate, a second 'glost' firing of glazed tiles. V&A.

Right: 5.47 A typical pillar-type dust-press for the production of tiles from powdered clay, manufactured by Wm. Boulton & Co. and illustrated by Furnival in 1904. Though representing the increasing use of machinery in the industry, such presses were nevertheless powered by hand using the large fly-wheel. Such

presses were the standard type throughout the nineteenth century, and although the first steam-powered presses were introduced in 1873 at Maw's, it was not until the twentieth century that semi- or fully automatic presses became standard. V&A.

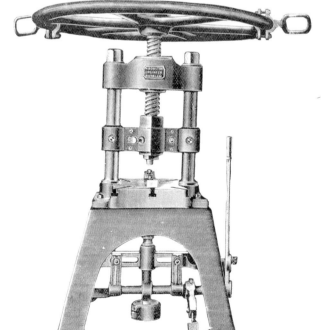

of blocks that followed the processes of production. At the rear of the site were the mill, slip-house and damping-house, in which the powdered clay was imparted with the correct degree of moisture. In front of these stood a long, three-storey workshop block: dust-pressed tiles and tesserae were made on the ground floor, inlaid tiles on the first. Cellars beneath provided storage for the prepared clay. Next came the hot-houses where the tiles were dried, saggar-houses where they were stacked in or removed from the large clay containers or 'saggars' which were loaded into the kiln, and the bottle ovens in which the tiles were fired. Lastly, an impressive block with a long and richly decorated street façade housed the offices, warehouses and showrooms.

Lynam went on to build major tileworks for Craven Dunnill & Co. in 1874 and for Maw & Co. in 1883, both at Jackfield, Shropshire. Once again, logical plans based around the processes of production were employed, with the proximity of rail transport for the delivery of raw materials and distribution of products also being fully exploited.

Omega and Bloomsbury

Opened in July 1913 at 33 Fitzroy Square in London, the Omega Workshops was a bold enterprise which brought colour, spontaneity and the sensibilities of Continental modern art to English interior design. Founded by the critic and painter Roger Fry, Omega made and sold a wide range of domestic items which were designed and produced by a group of young artists. The artists were employed for three half-days per week, and were required to work on an anonymous basis. Vanessa Bell and Duncan Grant were co-directors in the enterprise and were among the most prolific of the artists involved.

Pottery was produced by the workshops from the end of 1913, and an illustrated catalogue issued the following autumn listed the range of items by then available. This included tea sets, vases and bowls, as well as 'Tiles for Fireplaces painted to order'. Also in 1914, painted fireplace tiles were incorporated into the decorations of the Cadena Café in Westbourne Grove, London, one of a number of complete interior schemes carried out by the Workshops.

After the demise of Omega in 1919, Bell and Grant continued to produce domestic decorative items, often as part of interior design commissions. Tiles, which provided an ideal surface for their bold and lively painting style, were a regular product. These were painted by the artists at a pottery in south London and were sold individually or mounted in wooden frames for trays or tables. Furniture or fireplaces set with colourfully painted tiles were a feature of numerous interiors with which Bell and Grant were involved. These included their own home, Charleston Farmhouse, as well as Monk's House in Sussex, the home of Bell's sister, Virginia Woolf.

5.49 Duncan Grant's studio at Charleston, Sussex. The farmhouse was home to Grant and Vanessa Bell from 1916, and became a regular meeting place for the artists and writers associated with Bloomsbury. The interiors are an extraordinary expression of Grant and Bell's decorative style. Painted tiles feature in the fireplace.
© The Charleston Trust.

5.50 The interior of the Cadena Café in Westbourne Grove, as illustrated in the Omega Workshops catalogue of 1914. Omega was responsible for every aspect of the decorative scheme. The large fireplace is surrounded by a band of painted tiles.
V&A. L.2209-1955.

5.52 A panel of tin-glazed tiles depicting bathers, painted by Vanessa Bell in 1926. 46cm sq. V&A. C.22-1999.

Below: 5.51 Lytton Strachey in Repose, a panel of two tiles painted by Duncan Grant in the mid-1920s. The critic and biographer Lytton Strachey was a central figure of the Bloomsbury group, and a regular visitor to Charleston. Width 29.5cm. V&A. Misc.2:62-1934.

Right: 5.53 A tiled cast-iron stove, designed by Robert Medley and made by the Cozy Stove Co. Ltd. The tiles were designed and painted by Duncan Grant, probably in 1929. The stove was among the items in the collection of modern decorative art formed by Margaret Bulley under the guidance of Roger Fry. The collection was exhibited at the V&A in 1929 and was later given to the museum. V&A. Misc.2:63-1934.

Inlaid Tile Manufacture

The manufacture of an inlaid tile as practised today by Chris Cox of the Encaustic Tile Company in Jackfield: (a) The open wooden frame and plaster mould with which the tiles are formed; (b) Clay forming the background to the design is thumbed into the mould. In this case, a different clay to that forming the body of the tile is used, although this need not be the case. Additional colours can be added at this stage, if required; (c) The body clay is thrown into the mould;

(d) A hessian-covered wooden 'mawl' is used to tamp down the clay; (e) The back of the tile is scraped level; (f) The mould is pushed out from the frame and the tile lifted off; (g) Clay slip is poured into the impressions left by the mould; (h) Once dry, the surface of the tile is scraped level with a steel blade to reveal the design; (i) The edges of the tile, or in this case four small tiles, can be trimmed at this stage; (j) The tiles are allowed to dry further before firing.

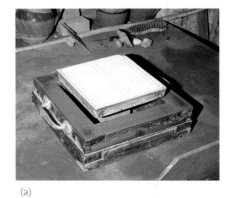

(a)

(b)

(c)

(d)

(e)

(f)

(g)

(h)

(i)

(j)

Bibliography

This bibliography is intended both to suggest further reading and to identify the sources used by the author in the preparation of the text. It has thus been organised thematically, following as closely as possible the structure of the book.

The following abbreviations have been used for frequently cited journals, catalogues and collected papers:

IduP: *Images du Pouvoir: Pavements du Faïence en France du XIIIe au XVIIe siècle*, Bourg-en-Bresse/Paris, 2000

JTACS: *Journal of the Tiles and Architectural Ceramics Society*

JBAA: *Journal of the British Archaeological Association*

La Ruta: *La Ruta de la Cerámica: Aproximación a la Historia de la Cerámica Arquitectonica*, Castellón, 2000

MNBM: Gaimster, D. (ed.), *Maiolica in the North: The Archaeology of Tin-Glazed Earthenware in North-West Europe c.1500–1600*, British Museum Occasional Paper No. 122, London, 1999

TCAMA: Deroeux, D. (ed.), *Terres Cuites Architecturales au MoyenAge*, Arras, 1986

Items marked * include an English translation.

CHAPTER 1

The literature on medieval tiles is vast. The most compendious publication on British tiles remains Eames' catalogue for the British Museum, though this should be read alongside more recent publications where appropriate. It also includes the most complete bibliography. The most complete bibliography of French tiles is that compiled by Norton.

General

Cherry, J., 'Pottery and tile', in Blair, J. and Ramsay, N., *English Medieval Industries*, London, 1991, pp189–209.

Eames, E., *Catalogue of Medieval Lead-glazed earthenware tiles in the Department of Medieval and Later Antiquities,* British Museum, London, 1980.

Eames, E., *English Tilers*, London, 1992.

Fawcett, J. (ed.), *Historic Floors: Their History and Conservation*, Oxford, 1998. For information on how tiled floors were laid, see p42.

Lane, A., *A Guide to the Collection of Tiles*, Victoria and Albert Museum, London, 1960, chapters 3 and 4.

Norton, E.C., 'De la couleur dans l'édifice médiéval: carreaux et carrelages gothiques. II. Les carreaux de pavage en France au moyen âge', *Revue de l'Art*, 63, 1984, pp59–72. On tile mosaic, see pp60–1.

Norton, C., 'Bibliographie des carreaux médiévaux Français', in *TCAMA*, pp321–48.

Norton, C., *Carreaux de Pavement du Moyen Age et de la Renaissance: Collections du musée Carnavalet*, Paris, 1992.

Shaw, H., *Specimens of Tile Pavements*, London, 1858.

Early relief and counter-relief tiles/Tile-mosaic

Biddle, M. and Kjølbye-Biddle, B., 'Floor Tiles' in *English Romanesque Art 1066–1200*, London, 1984, no.552. Discusses the twelfth-century tiles from St Albans Abbey.

Drury, P.J. and Norton, E.C., 'Twelfth-century floor- and roof-tiles at Orford Castle', *Proceedings of the Suffolk Institute of Archaeology and History*, 36 pt. I, 1987, pp1–7. Also contains a useful general outline of early developments in tile-making.

Gem, R. and Keen, L., 'Late Anglo-Saxon finds from the site of St Edmund's Abbey', *Proceedings of the Suffolk Institute of Archaeology*, XXXV, 1981, pp1–30.

Keen, L., 'Pre-conquest glazed relief tiles from All Saints Church, Pavement, York', *JBAA*, vol. CXLVI, 1993, pp67–86. On the dating of this series of tiles, see p81.

Norton, C., 'Early Cistercian tile pavements', in Norton, C. and Park, D. (eds), *Cistercian Art and Architecture in the British Isles*, Cambridge, 1986, pp228–55. On the incised and counter-relief series, see pp231–44; on tile-mosaic, see pp231 & 244–50.

Norton, C., 'Medieval Floor Tiles in Scotland', in Higgitt, J. (ed.), *Medieval Art and Architecture in the Diocese of St Andrews*, BAA Conference Transactions for the year 1986, 1994, pp137–73. See in particular pp137–41, in which the North Berwick tiles are discussed in the context of early European high-relief tiles. On tile-mosaic, see pp141–6.

Inlaid tiles and other tiles of the mid-thirteenth to fourteenth century

Cherry, J., 'The development of tile production in the north midlands of England', in *TCAMA*, pp227–33.

Cherry, J., 'Tiles', in Alexander, J. and Binski, P. (eds) *Age of Chivalry: Art in Plantagenet England 1200–1400*, London, 1987, pp181–2.

Drury, P.J. and Pratt, G.D., 'A late 13th and early 14th-century tile factory at Danbury, Essex', *Medieval Archaeology*, vol.19, 1975, pp92–164.

Drury, P.J., 'The production of brick and tile in medieval England', in Crossley, D.W. (ed.), *Medieval Industry*, CBA Research Report No. 40, 1981, pp126–42.

Eames, E., 'A tile pavement from the Queen's Chamber, Clarendon Palace, dated 1250–2', *JBAA*, vol. XX, 1957, pp95–106.

Eames, E., 'A thirteenth-century tiled pavement from the King's Chapel, Clarendon Palace', *JBAA*, vol. XXVI, 1963, pp40–50.

Hoekstra, T.J. and De Groot, H.L., 'Rectilinear mosaic tiled floors and tile production in Utrecht in the 14th century', in *TCAMA*, pp241–55.

Hohler, C., 'Medieval paving tiles in Buckinghamshire', *Records of Buckinghamshire*, vol. XIV, 1942, pp1–49 & 99–131. For the purchases of Penn tiles for royal building works, see pp6–7.

Janssen, H.L., 'Bricks, tiles and roofing-tiles in 's-Hertogenbosch during the middle ages', in *TCAMA*, pp73–93.

Landgraf, E., *Ornamentierte Bodenfliesen des Mittelalters in Süd- und Westdeutschland 1150–1550*, Stuttgart, 1993. The most comprehensive work on medieval German tiles.

Lewis, J.M., *Welsh Medieval Paving Tiles*, National Museum of Wales, Cardiff, 1976.

Monméja, J., 'Mosaïques du Moyen Age et carrelages émaillés à l'abbaye de Moissac', *Bulletin Archéologique*, 1894, pp189–206.

Norton, E.C., 'The medieval floor-tiles of Christchurch Priory', *Dorset Natural History and Archaeological Society Proceedings*, vol.102, 1980, pp49–64. On the Winchester-Clarendon series of the 1240s, see Group 1, p53; on the late thirteenth-century Wessex tiles, see Group 2, pp53–7.

Norton, E.C. and Horton, M.C., 'A Parisian workshop at Canterbury. A late thirteenth-century tile pavement in the Corona Chapel, and the origins of Tyler Hill', *JBAA*, CXXXIV, 1981, pp58–80.

Norton, C., 'The origins of two-coloured tiles in France and in England', in *TCAMA*, pp256–93.

Norton, C., 'The production and distribution of medieval floor tiles in France and England', in Altet, X.B.I., *Artistes, Artisans et Production Artistique au Moyen Age*, vol.III, Paris, 1990, pp101–31.

Norton, C., 'The medieval tile pavements of Winchester Cathedral', in Crook, J. (ed.), *Winchester Cathedral: Nine Hundred Years 1093–1993*, Winchester/Chichester, 1993, pp167–76.

Ramé, A., 'Etudes sur les carrelages émaillés, Saint-Pierre-sur-Dive', *Annales Archéologiques*, XII, 1852, pp282–93.

Stopford, J., 'The organisation of the medieval tile industry', *Oxford Journal of Archaeology*, 11(3), November, 1992, pp341–63.

Stopford, J., 'Modes of production among medieval tilers', *Medieval Archaeology*, vol. XXXVII, 1993, pp93–108.

Tile-stoves

Gaimster, D., Goffin, R. and Blackmore, L., 'The continental stove-tile fragments from St Mary Graces, London, in their British and European context', *Post-Medieval Archaeology*, vol. 24, 1990, pp1–49. For a general account of the tile-stove tradition in Europe, see pp4–16.

Gaimster, D.R.M., 'Post-medieval ceramic stove-tiles bearing the royal arms: evidence for their manufacture and use in southern Britain', *Archaeological Journal*, vol. 145, 1988, pp314–43.

Unger, I. (ed.), *Kölner Ofenkacheln. Die Bestände des Museums für Angewandt Kunst und des Kölnischen Stadtmuseums*, Cologne, 1988.

Later medieval tiles

Coleman-Smith, R. and Pearson, T., *Excavations in the Donyatt Potteries*, Chichester, 1998, pp323–7.

Eames, E., 'The Canynges pavement', *JBAA*, vol. XIV, 1951, pp33–46.

Horton, M.C., 'Imported motto tiles: a group of mid-sixteenth century slip-decorated Dutch floor tiles in England' in Detsicas, A. (ed.), *Collectanea Historica: Essays in Memory of Stuart Rigold*, Maidstone, 1981, pp235–46.

Keen, L., 'A series of seventeenth- and eighteenth-century lead-glazed relief tiles from north Devon', *JBAA*, vol. XXXII, 1969, pp144–70.

Kellock, A., 'Abbot Sebrok's pavement: a medieval tile floor in Gloucester Cathedral', *Transactions of the Bristol and Gloucestershire Archaeological Society*, 107, 1989, pp171–88.

Lewis, J.M., 'The logistics of transportation: a 15th-century example from south Wales', in *TCAMA*, pp234–40.

Norton, C., 'Medieval Floor Tiles in Scotland', in Higgitt, J. (ed.), *Medieval Art and Architecture in the Diocese of St Andrews*, BAA Conference Transactions for the year 1986, 1994, pp137–73. For a useful general discussion of plain tiles imported from the Netherlands, see pp150–3; similarly for imported patterned tiles see pp157–8.

CHAPTER 2

Spain

Algarra Pardo, V.M., 'Azulejería bajomedieval y tardomedieval Valenciana (siglos XIII–XV)', in *La Ruta*, pp66–73.*

Álvaro Zamora, M.I., 'Aportacíon Aragonesa a la cerámica de revestimento arquitectónico (siglos XIII–XVII)', in *La Ruta*, pp57–65.*

Anotonia Casanovas, M., 'Cerámica arquitectónica Catalána de época medieval y renacentista', in *La Ruta*, pp74–8.*

Coll Conesa, J., 'Talleres, técnicas y evolución de la azulejería medieval', in *La Ruta*, pp51–6.*

Dickie, J., 'The palaces of the Alhambra', in Dodds, J.D. (ed.), *Al-Andalus: The Art of Islamic Spain*, New York, 1992, pp134–51.

Gonzalez-Marti, M., *Cerámica del Levante Español*, 3 vols., Barcelona, 1944–52.

Martínez Caviró, B., *Cerámica Hispanomusulmana: Andalusí y Mudéjar*, Madrid, 1991.

Pleguezuelo Hernández, A., *Azulejo Sevillano: Catalogo del Museo de Artes y Costumbres Populares da Sevilla*, Sevilla, 1989.

Pleguezuelo, A., 'Azulejos de Sevilla' in *La Ruta*, pp42–50.*

Ray, A., *Spanish Pottery 1248–1898*, London, 2000.

Williams, B., 'Survey of Spanish tiles imported into England: an interim note', in Gerrard, C.M., Gutiérrez, A. and Vince, A.G. (eds), *Spanish Medieval Ceramics in Spain and the British Isles*, BAR International Series 610, Oxford, 1995, pp335–7.

Zozoya, J., 'Azulejos Islámicos en oriente y occidente', in *La Ruta*, pp38–41.*

Italy

Berti, F., 'Pavimentos y revestimentos esmaltados en Italia (siglos X–XVII)', in *La Ruta*, pp78–86.*

Whitehouse, D., 'The origins of Italian maiolica', *Archaeology*, vol. 31, no. 2, 1978, pp42–9.

France and the Low Countries

Bon, P., 'Aux marches du pouvoir: les sols armoriés de Jean de France, duc de Berry (1384–1416)', in *IduP*, pp56–64.

Démians d'Archimbaud, G. and Vallauri, L., 'Les carrelages en Provence, Comtat et Languedoc: des ateliers, des techniques et des oeuvres aux XIIe et XIVe siècles', in *IduP*, pp16–33.

Gagnière, S. and Thiriot, J., 'Aspects et provenances des carreaux de pavement du Palais des Papes d'Avignon au 14e siècle', in *TCAMA*, pp218–26.

Jugie, S., 'Les carreaux de faïence de Philippe le Hardi, duc de Bourgogne', in *IduP*, pp65–72.

Norton, C., 'Medieval tin-glazed painted tiles in north-west Europe', *Medieval Archaeology*, vol.28, 1984, pp133–72.

Norton, E.C., 'De l'Aquitaine à l'Artois: carreaux stannifères et carreaux plombifères des XIIIe et XIVe siècles en France', in *IduP*, pp34–48.

Rosen, J., 'La faïence française du XIIIe au XVIIe siècle', *Dossier de l'Art*, no. 70, October 2000. In particular, see pp6–19.

CHAPTER 3

Italy

Arbace, L., Middione, R. and Pagano, D.M., *Il Pavimento Maiolicato di San Giovanni a Carbonara*, Naples, 1998.

Baldisseri, G., *et. al.*, *Le Maioliche Cinquecentesche di Castelli: Una Grande Stagione Artistica Ritrovata*, 1989.* On the sixteenth-century ceiling tiles from the church of San Donato, see in particular Ricci, M., 'Renaissance Castelli maiolica from the origins to "compendiary" ware'; de Pompeis, V., 'Analysis of decorations and subdivision of the pottery type into groups'; and Donatone, G., 'The tiles from the original "cona" and XVI-century Castelli maiolica ware'. See also, Ricci, M., 'Sixteenth-century "comendiary" ware and wares decorated on coloured grounds'.

Bandini, G., 'Profilo per una storia degli impianti maiolicati italiani (1400–1550)' in de Norden, I., *et. al.* (eds), *Azulejos: As Metamorfoses do Azul / Le Metamorfosi dell'Azzurro*, Paris, 1995, pp34–54.

Berardi, P., *L'Antica Maiolica di Pesaro Dal XIV al XVII Secolo*, Florence, 1984. See pp18–19 for the date of the pavement of the Vaselli chapel, and pp207–9 for the attribution of that of the Convento di San Paolo.

Berti, F., 'Pavimentos y revestimentos esmaltados en Italia (siglos X–XVII)', in *La Ruta*, pp78–86.*

Casali, M.P.G., 'Ceramic tiles for the Gonzaga', in Chambers, D. and Martineau, J., *Splendours of the Gonzaga*, London, 1981, pp44–5. See also pp173–4.

Fiocci, C. and Gherardi, G., *La Ceramica di Deruta dal XIII al XVIII Secolo/Deruta Pottery from the 13th to the 18th century*, Perugia, 1994, pp113–20.*

Fiocci, C. and Gherardi, G., 'Considerazioni su un pavimento di stile durantino a Perugia', in Wilson, T. (ed.), *Italian Renaissance Pottery*, London, 1990, pp96–100.

Gardelli, G., *Maiolica per l'Architettura: Pavimenti e Rivestimenti Rinascimentali di Urbino e del Suo Territorio*, Urbino, 1993.

Lane, Arthur, *A Guide to the Collection of Tiles*, Victoria and Albert Museum, London, 1960, chapter 5.

Mallet, J.V.G., 'In Botega di Maestro Guido Durantino in Urbino', *Burlington Magazine*, 1987, pp284–98. Includes a discussion of the commissioning of tiles by Giralomo Genga from a consortium of Urbino potters.

Mallet, J.V.G., 'Tiled floors and court designers in Mantua and northern Italy', in *The Court of the Gonzaga in the Age of Mantegna*, Rome, n.d. [c.1997], pp253–72.

Poole, J.E., *Italian Maiolica and Incised Slipware in the Fitzwilliam Museum, Cambridge*, Cambridge, 1995, pp197–8, 275 and 283–4.

Quinterio, F., *Maiolica Nell'Architettura del Rinascimento Italiano (1440–1520)*, Firenze, n.d. [c.1990–1].

Rackam, Bernard, *Catalogue of Italian Maiolica*, Victoria and Albert Museum, London, 1940.

Ravanelli Guidotti, 'Il pavimento della cappella Vaselli in San Petronio a Bologna: bilancio del suo studio complessivo', *Atti XXI Convegno Internazionale della Ceramica "Rivestimenti Parietali e Pavimentali dal Medievo Al Liberty" II*, 1988, pp245–54.

Schianchi, L.F., *Ai Piedi della Badessa: Un Pavimento Maiolicato per Maria De Benedetti Badessa de S. Paolo dal 1471 al 1482*, Parma, 1988.*

Wilson, T., *et. al.*, *La Sistina della Maiolica*, Colledara, 1993.* Discusses the seventeenth-century ceiling tiles of the church of San Donato, Castelli.

Wilson, T., 'Italian maiolica around 1500: some considerations on the background to Antwerp maiolica', in *MNBM*, pp5–21.

Hungary
Voit, P. and Holl, I., *Old Hungarian Stove Tiles*, Budapest, 1963. For the *maiolica* floor tiles produced for Matthias Corvinus, see pp27–31.

Antwerp and England
Bart, J.M., 'North Netherlands Maiolica of the sixteenth century', in *MNBM*, pp125–36.

Betts, I., 'Early tin-glazed floor tile production in London', in *MNBM*, pp173–4.

Britton, F., *London Delftware*, London, 1987. For Antwerp and the Andries family, see pp18–22.

Dumortier, C., 'Les faïenciers italiens à Anvers au XVIe siècle, aspects historiques', *Faenza*, LXXIII, 4–6, 1987, pp161–72.

Dumortier, C., 'Des majoliques d'Anvers aux faïences de Delft', *Salon International de la Céramique de Collection et des Arts du Feu*, Paris, 1997, pp31–7.*

Dumortier, C., 'Maiolica production in Antwerp: the documentary evidence', in *MNBM*, pp107–11.

Dumortier, C., 'Pavements en majolique Anversoise au temps de Marguerite d'Austriche', in *IduP*, pp98–105.

Gaimster, D. and Hughes, M., 'South Netherlands maiolica floor tiles from the Broad Arrow Tower, Tower of London', in *MNBM*, pp175–9.

Gaimster, D. and Hughes, M., 'The earliest maiolica stove in north-west Europe: re-analysis of the Dissolution finds from the abbey of St Mary Graces, London', in *MNBM*, pp185–8.

Hurst, J.G., 'Sixteenth-century South Netherlands maiolica imported into Britain and Ireland', in *MNBM*, pp91–106.

Veeckman, J., 'Maiolica in sixteenth- and early seventeenth-century Antwerp: the archaeological evidence', in *MNBM*, pp113–23.

France
Brut, C., 'Les pavements de faïence du château des rois de France', in *IduP*, pp163–4.

Crépin-Leblond, T., 'La renaissance Française', in *IduP*, pp148–62.

Crépin-Leblond, T., 'Pavements épiscopaux de la fin du XVe siècle', in *IduP*, pp76–81.

Démians d'Archimbaud, G. and Vallauri, L., 'Les tapis bleus et blancs dans la vallée du Rhône; un style Valencien, une origine incertaine', in *IduP*, pp74–5.

Mallet, J.V.G., 'Tiled floors and court designers in Mantua and northern Italy', in *The Court of the Gonzaga in the Age of Mantegna*, Rome, n.d. [c.1997], pp253–72. Discusses gifts from the Grand Duke Cosimo II of Tuscany to Maria de Medici.

Nivière, M-D., 'Le pavement de faïence de l'eglise de Brou: état de la question', in *IduP*, pp119–33.

Rosen, J., 'Entre le moyen âge et la Renaissance: le(s) pavement(s) du château de Longecourt-en-Plaine (1495)', in *IduP*, pp82–92.

Rosen, J., 'La faïence française du XIIIe au XVIIe siècle', *Dossier de l'Art*, no. 70, October 2000. In particular, see pp20–47 and 56–65.

Roudier, J-M., 'Les pavements Nivernais des origines jusqu'au mileu du XVIIe siècle', in *IduP*, pp169–79.

Spain
Frothingham, A.W., *Tile Panels of Spain 1500–1650*, New York, 1969.

Maroto Garrido, M., 'Aplicaciones arquitectónicas de la cerámica de Talavera: sus influencias y expansión' in *La Ruta*, pp106–11.*

Pleguezuelo, A., 'Azulejos de Sevilla' in *La Ruta*, pp42–50.*

Ray, A., 'Francisco Niculoso called Pisano', in Wilson, T. (ed.), *Italian Renaissance Pottery: papers written in association with a colloquium at the British Museum in 1987*, London, 1990, pp261–6.

Ray, A., *Spanish Pottery 1248–1898*, London, 2000.

Genoa and Sicily

Berendsen, A., *et. al.*, *Tiles: A General History*, London, 1967, pp88–90.

Farris, G. and Raffo, C., 'Un inedito pannello Genovese cinquecentesco in maiolica', *Faenza*, no.5–6, 1995, pp250–4.

Marzinot, F., *Ceramica e Ceramisti di Liguria*, Genoa, 1979.

Ragona, A., *La maiolica siciliana dalle origini all'ottocento*, Palermo, 1975.

Portugal

Monteiro, J.P., 'Algunos aspectos sobre la utilación del azulejo en Portugal', in *La Ruta*, pp100–5.*

Pereira, J.C-B., *Portuguese Tiles from the National Museum of Azulejo, Lisbon*, 1995.

Sabo, R. and Falcato, J.N., *Portuguese Decorative Tiles: Azulejos*, New York, 1998.

CHAPTER 4

The Netherlands

Bentz, B., *et. al.*, *Châteaux de Faïence: XIVe–XVIIIe siècle*, Marly-le-Roi, 1993.

Berendsen, A., *et. al.*, *Tiles: A General History*, London, 1967. The extensive coverage of Dutch tiles in this book remains useful, particularly on export and influence abroad.

Dam, J.D. van, Tichelaar, P.J. and Schaap, E., *Dutch Tiles in the Philadlephia Museum of Art*, Philadelphia, 1984. A useful catalogue with excellent introductory essays on both history and production techniques.

Dam, J.D. van, 'Het verschil tussen droge en natte massabereiding van klei en het effect op de Nederlandse tegel', *Vormen uit Vuur*, 1, 1992, pp7–9 and 26. English summary. Discusses the advantages of 'washing the clay'.

Dam, J.D. van, 'Delfts uit de provincie: aardewerk uit Hollandse tegelfabriken/Delftware from the Province: earthenware from tile factories in Holland', *Vormen uit Vuur*, 168/9, 1999. English summary.

Erkelens, A.M.L.E., *'Delffs Porcelijn' van koningin Mary II: Ceramiek op Het Loo uit de tijd van Willem III en Mary II/Queen Mary's 'Delft Porcelain': Ceramics at Het Loo from the time of William and Mary*, Apeldoorn, 1996. See in particular pp22–7 and 33–4.*

Hawkins, E. (ed.), *Travels in Holland etc,1634–5 by Sir William Brereton, Bart*, Chetham Society, 1844.

Jonge, C.H. de, *Dutch Tiles*, New York, 1971.

Lane, A., 'Daniel Marot: designer of Delft vases and of gardens at Hampton Court', *Connoisseur*, CXXIII, March 1949, pp19–24.

Lemmen, H. van, *Delftware Tiles*, London, 1997.

Oldenziel, R., 'De tegelbakkerij Van der Kloet in Amsterdam, 1686–1808: een grensoverschrijdende firma/The Van der Kloet tile factory in Amsterdam, 1686–1808', *Vormen uit Vuur*, 1, 1992, pp16–32 and 49–51. English summary.

Paape, G., *De Plateelbakker of Delftsch Aardewerkmaaker*, Amsterdam, 1978 (originally Dordrecht, 1794).

Pluis, J., *De Nederlandse Tegel: decors en benamingen 1570–1930/The Dutch Tile: Designs and Names 1570–1930*, Leiden, 1997.*

Schaap, E.B., *Bloemen op Tegels in de Gouden Eeuw van prent tot tegel/Dutch Floral Tiles in the Golden Age and their Botanical Prints*, Haarlem, 1994.*

Schama, S., *The Embarrassment Of Riches: An Interpretation Of Dutch Culture In The Golden Age*, London, 1987. On the affordability of tiles, see pp317–18.

Tichelaar, P.J., 'Nederelandse tegels en tegeltableaus op het Iberisch schiereiland/Dutch tiles and tile pictures in the Iberian peninsula', *Vormen uit Vuur*, 1, 1992, pp6–15 and 49. English summary.

Portugal

Meco, J., *Azulejos de Portugal: Séculos XVII e XVIII: Rota da Asia/Portuguese Tiles in the 17th and 18th Centuries: The Asian Route*, Lisbon, 1991.*

See also citations for Chapter 3.

Spain

Giral Quintana, M.D., 'Los azulejos Catalanes policromos de los siglos XVII, XVIII y XIX', in *La Ruta*, pp126–30.*

Pérez Guillén, I.V., 'La azulejería Valenciana de los siglos XVII, XVIII y XIX', in *La Ruta*, pp112–22.*

Pleguezuelo, A., 'Azulejos de Sevilla' in *La Ruta*, pp42–50.*

Ray, A., *Spanish Pottery 1248–1898*, London, 2000.

Townsend, J., *A Journey through Spain in the Years 1786 and 1787*, London, 1791.

Italy

Donatone, G., *Pavimenti e Rivestimenti Maiolicati in Campania*, Napoli, 1981.

Donatone, G., *Riggiola Napoletana: Pavimenti e Rivestimenti Maiolicati dal Seicento all'Ottocento*, 1997.

Germany, France, Scandinavia and Russia

Berendsen, A., *et. al.*, *Tiles: A General History*, London, 1967, pp229–36.

Lemmen, H. van, *Delftware Tiles*, London, 1997, pp131–42.

Ovsiannikov, I.U., *Russkie izraztsy/Russian Tiles*, Leningrad, 1968. English summary.

United Kingdom

Archer, M., *Delftware: The Tin-Glazed Earthenware of the British Isles - A Catalogue of the Collection in the Victoria and Albert Museum*, London, 1997. Includes excellent essays on the production and use of tiles.

Britton, F., *London Delftware*, London, 1987. Includes detailed factory histories.

Cox, A. and Cox, A., *Rockingham Pottery and Porcelain*, 1983, p46. Details the supply of creamware tiles by Greens Bingley & Co.

Horne, J., *English Tin-Glazed Tiles*, London, 1989.

Kelly, A., *Decorative Wedgwood in Architecture and Furniture*, London, 1965, pp119–24.

Mayer, J., *History of the Art of Pottery in Liverpool*, Liverpool, 1855, p26.

Ray, A., *English Delftware Tiles*, London, 1973.

Ray, A., *Liverpool Printed Tiles*, London, 1994.

Ray, A., 'Staffordshire Tiles 1750–1840', *Transactions of the English Ceramic Circle*, vol. 15, part 2, 1994, pp194–204.

Robinson, J.M., *Georgian Model Farms: A Study of Decorative and Model Farm Buildings in the Age of Improvement, 1700–1846*, Oxford, 1983. An excellent account of decorative dairies is on pp92–100.

CHAPTER 5

Much of the most reliable information is in the contemporary accounts of Furnival and Jewitt. Many useful articles on nineteenth- and twentieth-century tiles are to be found in the *Journal of the Tiles and Architectural Ceramics Society*, as well as in that society's more regular publication, *Glazed Expressions.*

Nineteenth century

Atterbury, P. & Irvine, L., *The Doulton Story*, Stoke-on-Trent, 1979.

Atterbury, P. and Wainwright, C. (eds), *Pugin: A Gothic Passion*, New Haven/London, 1994, pp143–9.

Baker, D., *Potworks: The Industrial Archaeology of the Staffordshire Potteries*, London, 1991. See in particular pp60–83.

Beaulah, G.K., 'Samuel Wright of Shelton and his tiles', *JTACS*, vol. 3, 1990, pp28–32.

Catleugh, J., *William de Morgan Tiles*, London, 1983.

Cross, A.J., *Pilkington's Royal Lancastrian Pottery and Tiles*, London, 1980.

Estall i Poles, V. and Luis Porcar, J., 'El desarrollo industrial y technológico durante el siglo XIX hasta el primer tercio del siglo XX', in *La Ruta*, pp144–54.*

Estall i Poles, V.J., *Catálogo de la Colección de Azulejos de Serie del Siglo XIX*, Castellón, n.d. [2000].

Fawcett, J. (ed.), *Historic Floors: Their History and Conservation*, Oxford, 1998. For the Palace of Westminster, see A.T. Jardine's account, pp187–93.

Furnival, W.J., *Leadless Decorative Tiles, Faience and Mosaic*, Stone, 1904. Includes Ambrose Wood's account of tilework design, pp801–13.

Godden, G.A., *Chamberlain-Worcester Porcelain 1788–1852*, London, 1982. See pp287–8 on Chamberlain's encaustic tiles. A facsimile of 'A day at the royal porcelain-works, Worcester', from *The Penny Magazine*, February 1843, is on pp361–8.

Greene, B., 'The Godwins of Hereford', *JTACS*, vol. 1, 1982, pp8–16.

Hawkins Opie, J., 'Tiles and tableware', in Parry, L. (ed.), *William Morris*, London, 1996, pp180–97.

Herbert, T., 'Jackfield encaustic tile works', *Glazed Expressions*, no. 23, 1991, pp9–10.

Herbert, T. and Huggins, K., *The Decorative Tile in Architecture and Interiors*, London, 1995.

Jewitt, L., *The Ceramic Art of Great Britain*, London, 1878. See in particular vol.I, pp258, 305–17 and vol.II, pp192, 195–206, 213–18, 228–32, 256, 260–1, 452.

Jones, J., *Minton: The First Two Hundred Years of Design and Production*, Shrewsbury, 1993, pp159–85 and 215–33.

Kay, G., 'Charles Lynam – an architect of tile factories', *JTACS*, vol. 4, 1992, pp21–8.

Lemmen, H. van, *Tiles in Architecture*, London, 1993. A useful general history, particularly strong on the nineteenth century.

Lemmen, H. van and Verbrugge, B.G., *Art Nouveau Tiles*, London, 1999.

Lockett, T.A., *Collecting Victorian Tiles*, Woodbridge, 1979.

Long, H., *The Edwardian House: The Middle-Class Home in Britain 1880–1914*, Manchester, 1993. On bathrooms, see pp95–8; on fireplaces see pp101–15; on tiled walls and floors, see pp147–52.

Maillard, A., *La Céramique Architecturale 1880–1930: Paris,*

Normandie, Beauvaisis, Paris, 1995.

Muthesius, H., *Das Englische Haus*, Berlin, 1904–5 (*The English House*, Oxford, 1987).

Myers, R. and H., *William Morris Tiles*, Shepton Beauchamp, 1996.

Nichols, J.G., *Examples of Decorative Tiles sometimes termed Encaustic*, London, 1845. Includes volumes previously published as *Examples of Inlaid Gothic Tiles.*

Physick, J., *The Victoria and Albert Museum: The History of its Building*, Oxford, 1982, pp124–42.

Pleguezuelo, A., 'Azulejos de Sevilla' in *La Ruta*, pp42–50.*

Porter, V., 'William De Morgan and the Islamic tiles of Leighton House', *Decorative Arts Society Journal*, no.16, 1992, pp76–9.

Porter, V., *Islamic Tiles*, London, 1995. See in particular pp120–1.

Reed, C., 'A discovery in Pennsylvania: the "tiles" guardbook of John Gough Nichols', *JTACS*, vol. 6, 1996, pp3–12.

Reynolds, J.S., 'Alfred Reynolds and the block process', *JTACS*, vol. 5, 1994, pp20–6.

Scott, G.G., *On the Conservation of Ancient Architectural Monuments and Remains: A Paper Read Before the Royal Institute of British Architects, January 6th, 1862*, Oxford/London, 1864.

Skinner, D.S. and Lemmen, H. van (eds), *Minton Tiles 1835–1935*, Stoke-on-Trent Art Gallery and Museum, 1984.

Victoria and Albert Museum, *Catalogue of Works by William De Morgan*, London, 1921. Includes a useful technical account supplied by Halsey Ricardo.

'New tile works, Stoke-upon-Trent', *The Builder*, 27 March 1869, p249. An account of the new Minton Hollins factory.

Twentieth century

Carter, C. and Hidden, H.R., *Wall and Floor Tiling*, London, 1951.

Collins, J., 'Roger Fry's social vision of art', in Green, C. (ed.), *Art Made Modern: Roger Fry's Vision of Art*, London, 1999, pp73–84. A useful brief discussion of the Omega Workshops.

Doulton and Company, *Pictures in Pottery: a note on some hospital wall decorations recently executed by Doulton and Company*, London, 1904.

Greene, J., *Brightening the Long Days*, Gloucester, 1987.

Hamilton, D., *The Thames and Hudson Manual of Architectural Ceramics*, London, 1978.

Hawkins, J., *The Poole Potteries*, London, 1980.

Hawkins Opie, J., *Scandinavia: Ceramics and Glass in the Twentieth Century*, London, 1989.

Hayward, L. and Atterbury, P., *Poole Pottery: Carter & Company and their Successors 1873–1995*, Shepton Beauchamp, 1995.

Lemmen, H. van and Blanchett, C., *20th Century Tiles*, Princes Risborough, 1999.

Myers, L., 'Variety and vitality in ceramic tiles', *Design*, 195, March 1965, pp28–35.

Omega Workshops Ltd: Artist Decorators, nd [1914]. The same catalogue appears also to have been issued under the title 'Omega Workshops Descriptive Catalogue'.

Ramakers, R. and Bakker, G. (eds), *Droog Design: Spirit of the Nineties*, Rotterdam, 1998, pp77–84.

Tatton Brown, W., 'Tile-work today', in *The Architectural Review Supplement*, May 1939, pp265-8.

Willis, A., 'Tiles take off', *Studio Pottery Ceramics in Society*, 35, Spring 1999, pp.23–37.

Index